EDGEWORK

EDGEWORK

. . . .

CRITICAL ESSAYS ON KNOWLEDGE AND POLITICS

Wendy Brown

PRINCETON UNIVERSITY PRESS

PRINCETON AND OXFORD

Library of Congress Cataloging-in-Publication Data

Brown, Wendy.
Edgework : critical essays on knowledge and politics / Wendy Brown.
p. cm.
Includes bibliographical references and index.
ISBN-10: 0-691-12360-8 (cloth : alk. paper)
ISBN-13: 978-0-691-12360-8 (cloth : alk. paper)
1. Political science.   2. Feminist theory.   I. Title.
JA71.B758 2005
20'.1'10823—dc22   2005050497

British Library Cataloging-in-Publication Data is available

This book has been composed in Palatino Typeface
Printed on acid-free paper. ∞
pup.princeton.edu
Printed in the United States of America

1   3   5   7   9   10   8   6   4   2

CONTENTS

PREFACE

E ACH of these essays was written for a particular occasion: a conference keynote address, a topical anthology, a special issue of a journal. Such occasions mimic, in certain ways, the experience of the political realm: one is challenged to think here, now, about a problem that is set and framed by someone else, and to do so before a particular audience or in dialogue with others not of one's own choosing. These conditions bear enough similarities to some of the constraints and demands of thinking that must respond to given political circumstances to offer good practice for political theorists, who are often removed from the unique rhythms and constraints of political life. Moreover, as these occasions productively divert scholars from our own research questions, they free us to think more broadly, more speculatively, and more dialogically than usual.

As critiques of particular discursive, institutional, or political practices, these essays are endeavors in what Foucault termed the "local character of criticism" he considered appropriate to post-Enlightenment thinking.[1] Local criticism, which Foucault paired with the emergence of the "specific intellectual" (contrasted with the universal intellectual), resets the compass points of critical theory that are derived from its Kantian-Hegelian-Marxist heritage. It replaces critique of an imagined social totality and an ambition of total transformation with critique of historically specific and local constellations of power and an ambition to refigure political possibility against the seeming givenness of the present. While these replacements are sometimes disapprovingly read as a retreat from universal, normative, and politically revolutionary investments, such disappointment makes sense only if one remains gripped by the ontological and epistemological premises whose very critique has occasioned the shift away from social totalities and universal norms. If one instead rejects the idea that social orders are unified and bounded, that they are organized and moved by a single kind of power, that this power can be grasped and replaced to achieve emancipatory social transformation, that this power can be theorized objectively, and that social and political theory are thus appropriate candidates for science, then local criticism, rather than downgrading the project of critical theory, articulates potency and humility vis-à-vis both the complex powers producing the present and the difficult task of apprehending this present. From this perspective, critical theory becomes more radical *and* more efficacious as it surrenders universal and comprehensive aspirations, as it engages historically and culturally specific powers, problems, and knowledges.

Each of these essays begins with a concrete problem: for example, the relationship of loyalty, love, and dissent in contemporary American political life; the emergence of neoliberal rationality as a form of governmentality; the current intellectual disorientation of women's studies programs; or the identity crisis of political theory in relation to recent historical disseminations of the political and the theoretical. Such problems are rendered as markers of political or intellectual landscapes themselves in need of rethinking in order to articulate political possibilities beyond those offered by the existing discursive framing of the problem. The purpose is not to reveal the Truth of a particular problematic, or to "get to the bottom" of it. Rather, the point is to critically interrogate the framing and naming practices, challenge the dogmas (including those of the Left and of feminism), and discern the constitutive powers shaping the problem at hand. Boundaries, naming practices, dogmas, and constitutive powers are among the objects of local criticism; interrogation, challenge, discernment, and displacement are among its actions. These relatively modest objects and practices offer an alternative to the more grandiose ones of an earlier instantiation of critical theory, in which what was at stake was nothing less than apprehending systems and totalities; identifying essential principles, powers, or sources of historical movement; and providing the key to their overcoming.

The essays assembled in this volume traverse, and in some cases link, disparate intellectual orbits and idioms—for example, political theory and women's studies, or left activists and liberal scholars of politics. It is my hope that when they are read as a collection, these relatively distinct communities might consider new ways of engaging their own dilemmas by considering how they take shape elsewhere. Another line of division between these essays is that some were prepared as public addresses while others were conceived from the beginning as contributions to written symposia even if they were first delivered as papers. In the case of chapters 1 and 6, I have chosen to leave their talk style intact, since, in addition to informality, the medium elicits potentially politically useful qualities of urgency and insistence.

The first three essays were written for events focused on the sea change in political concerns and political consciousness in the aftermath of September 11. "Untimeliness and Punctuality" was the keynote address for a 2004 conference of political theory graduate students titled "Critical Theory in Dark Times." "Political Idealization and Its Discontents" was written for a 2002 seminar, "Dissent in Dangerous Times," a convocation of liberal and left scholars of American law and politics responding to the immediate post-9/11 chill in American public discourse. And "Neoliberalism and the End of Liberal Democracy" was first offered to a 2003 symposium titled "The Left, After . . . ," which aimed to consider the thinking and practice of the American Left two years after 9/11.

The fourth essay, "At the Edge," responded to an invitation to reflect on the present and future of political theory at a session of the American Political Science Association annual meeting titled "What Is Political Theory Today?" The fifth essay, "Freedom's Silences," pivots between the more generic contexts of the preceding essays and the forthrightly feminist ones of the two that follow. "Freedom's Silences" was presented at a set of events on censorship sponsored by the Getty Institute; originally prepared for a conference titled "Silencing Women: Feminism(s), Censorship, and Difference," it was also presented at the final gathering in the series, "Censorship and Silencing: Practices of Cultural Regulation," which cast a wider net over the problem of censorship.

The last two essays were written in response to calls for critical reflection by feminist scholars on past and current feminist projects. Their occasions were framed by a related set of provocations suggesting (as their titles underscored) that feminism or gender studies was in crisis, or at a critical turning point. "Feminism Unbound" was the keynote for a United Kingdom Women's Studies Network conference on the topic "Beyond Sex and Gender? The Future of Women's Studies." And "The Impossibility of Women's Studies" was written for a special issue of the feminist theory journal *Differences*, titled *Women's Studies at the Edge*.

Not all of these offerings were joyously or gratefully received by their original audiences. In particular, the essays on feminist theory and feminist studies were angrily rebuffed by some listeners and readers. This is not the place to diagnose such rebuffs, which cannot be distilled into a single position. But several points dealt with at greater length in the essays themselves are worth emphasizing: namely, that critique is not equivalent to rejection or denunciation, that the call to rethink something is not inherently treasonous but can actually be a way of caring for and even renewing the object in question, and that the experience of being riled by a theoretical utterance, and especially of being provoked to anger or defensiveness, can sometimes spark a line of rich reflection. There is perhaps no more productive incitation for critical thinkers than the unwelcome disturbance of settled convictions and no more useless demeanor for critical theory than that of complacent attachment or defensive righteousness.

Acknowledgments

I am indebted to seven individuals whose invitations originally occasioned these essays—Chris Connery, Shirin Deylami, Robert Post, Austin Sarat, Joan Wallach Scott, Stephen White, and Marysia Zalewski. Individual essays benefited from criticism by Judith Butler, Bill Connolly, Tom Dumm, Carla Freccero, Janet Halley, Val Hartouni, Gail Hershatter, Robert Meister, Helene Moglen, and Joan W. Scott. Bonnie Honig read the entire manuscript and offered excellent suggestions for revision. Robyn Marasco assisted in preparing the final manuscript. Colleen Pearl meticulously proofed and indexed. Alice Falk, copyeditor extraordinaire, has once again unknotted my prose, curtailed my syntactical license, and searched out inconsistency in the most minute details. Ian Malcolm, my editor at Princeton University Press for many years now, is the soul of integrity and discernment in publishing.

Chapters 2, 6, and 7 appear essentially unrevised from their original published form. Chapters 3, 4, and 5 have been modestly revised. Chapter 1 has not been previously published. Permission to reprint has been granted as follows: "Political Idealization and Its Discontents," Austin Sarat, ed., *Dissent in Dangerous Times* (University of Michigan Press, 2005); "Neo-Liberalism and the End of Liberal Democracy," *Theory and Event* 7.1, Fall 2003; "At the Edge," *Political Theory* 30.4, August 2002; "Freedom's Silences," Robert Post, ed., *Censorship and Silencing* (Getty Research Institute, 1998); "Feminism Unbound: Revolution, Mourning, Politics," *Parallax*, Spring 2003; and "The Impossibility of Women's Studies," *Differences: A Journal of Feminist Cultural Studies*, Fall 1998.

EDGEWORK

ONE

■ ■ ■ ■

UNTIMELINESS AND PUNCTUALITY:
CRITICAL THEORY IN DARK TIMES

> Criticism is not an "homage" to the truth of the past or to the truth
> of "others"—it is a construction of the intelligibility
> of our own time.
> —ROLAND BARTHES, "What Is Criticism?"

THIS ESSAY reflects on timeliness and untimeliness in critical political theory. It works outside the intellectual circuits through which both problems are conventionally routed—those offered by Kant, Hegel, Heidegger, and the Frankfurt School—in order to feature aspects of the relationship between political time and critique overshadowed by these traditions of thought. Foucault once defined critique as "the art of not being governed quite so much,"[1] and these reflections might be taken in the spirit of a refusal to be governed quite so much by critical theory's traditional intellectual signposts. They accord, too, with Benjamin's counsel to "wrest tradition away from a conformism that is about to overpower it," a wresting Benjamin thought could be enabled through igniting images of the past different from those the present routinely paints for or as itself.[2]

We begin with three tales from contemporary political life, each of which poses a conundrum for the time of critique.

1. The "Geneva Accords," an unofficial framework for a peace settlement between Palestinians and Israeli Jews, were signed amid much fanfare by selected Palestinian and Israeli representatives in December 2003. Designed to model what "the people" wanted and could agree on (as opposed to what intransigent official leadership would do) and

to represent a replacement of earlier negotiation processes, including the Oslo Accords, the Geneva Accords mapped in considerable detail a contemporary two-state solution to the enduring, bloody conflict in the Middle East.

Both committed Zionists and Palestinian militants rejected the Geneva Accords as selling out their interests. Ariel Sharon condemned the document out of hand, and even Labor Party Prime Minister Ehud Barak heaped scorn on it. Most Palestinian organizations also rejected it. In addition, many progressives committed to a just peace in the Middle East viewed the accords as representing compromises of Palestinian aspirations and entitlements too great to swallow: they largely gave up the Palestinian right of return (leaving the matter for Israel alone to determine), left intact a number of Jewish settlements (including those around East Jerusalem), and more generally represented significant Israeli incursions into Palestinian territory. In addition, for many committed democrats, the time of the two-state solution, if it had ever existed, had passed, for practical as well as principled reasons. Such critics argued that the aspiration for democracy and peace in the Middle East required a reckoning with the antidemocratic heart of a Zionist state that is also a colonial one, and insisted on the importance of formulating a binational state that would harbor Palestinians and Jews on a one-person, one-vote basis.

Critics in this last group were themselves harshly condemned by supporters of the Geneva Accords. In essence the condemnation ran: "You are holding out for utopia while we are modeling real-world solutions. If you truly care about peace in the Middle East, then you must support the accords. If you do not support them, you care more about your abstract ideals than about politics."

2. Once John Kerry emerged as the clear nominee of the Democratic Party for the 2004 presidential elections, Ralph Nader threw his hat into the ring. While delighting Republicans, Nader's move infuriated most liberals and leftists, including many who had voted for Nader in 2000. "Anybody but Bush" was the cry of the day, which meant that every voter had to line up behind the emerging Democratic Party nominee, whatever one's misgivings about him. Nader was a selfish spoiler, fit for nothing more than denunciation.

A few small voices, however, suggested that Nader was doing what he has always done: namely, working publicly to remind America that obscenely gerrymandered political districts and two corporately financed political parties do not a democracy make.[3] What was the harm of this reminder when Nader knows full well that we all—perhaps even Nader himself—would vote for Kerry in November? And if not during election season, when else could this point be made as powerfully and vividly? What if Nader's candidacy were to make Kerry even slightly more accountable to the citizenry and less beholden to corporate interests? Above all, what if Nader's candidacy, based largely on a critique of the corrupt and antidemocratic aspects of the existing electoral and party system, became a way to infiltrate the media lockout of such critique?

3. In early January 2004, recently elected Mayor Gavin Newsom of San Francisco declared that the city would commence granting marriage licenses to same-sex partners. In the ensuing weeks, as thousands of lesbian and gay couples descended on San Francisco's City Hall, other cities in California and in New York, New Jersey, and Oregon jumped on the bandwagon. Suddenly, gay marriage was the civil rights issue of the day. The marriages themselves were compared by liberal pundits to the bus and lunch-counter boycotts of the black civil rights movement. The *New York Times* gave gay marriage a ringing endorsement and, along with scores of other American newspapers and magazines, carried joyous pictures and stories of gay couples tying the knot. When, after four weeks, the California Supreme Court ruled against Newsom's initiative and halted San Francisco's issuance of marriage licenses to same-sex couples, San Francisco's gay district, the Castro, exploded. Under the slogan "We demand the equal right to marry," demonstrators rallied and chanted through the night.

Meanwhile, those who were dubious about either the egalitarian or emancipatory aspects of the right to marry—whether from feminist, queer, left, or anti-statist perspectives—were largely reduced to silence. So much as mentioning that marriage has functioned historically to secure women's subordination and male privilege, to hoard wealth and transmit property, and to regulate sexuality, ethnicity, race, class, and nation was tantamount to throwing dirt in the punch bowl. Just as unmentionable was the fact that as a state- and religiously granted "status," marriage itself buttresses the intermingled power and authority of church and state, which together secure and regulate marriage as *the* legitimate modality for love, for sex, and for child rearing. Equally unspeakable was the suggestion that gays and lesbians promulgating marriage as the ultimate sanctification of love between two people were biting from the same mythohistorical muffin as anti-gay conservatives declaring marriage to be timeless and transcendent in meaning. If this was a civil rights battle, there was no room to cast doubt or aspersion on the value or the meaning of the right being fought for. It is therefore hardly surprising that when a threesome unsuccessfully sought a marriage license from San Francisco city officials, they were jeered by their fellow queers: "You're ruining it for all of us," yelled the wedding-besotted crowd as the triplet of sexual deviants walked away from the courthouse.

Despite the variation in their political significance, these three political episodes feature a common conservative and moralizing rejection of critique as untimely. "It is not the time," declare the workers in the political trenches to the critics, a retort that invokes *time* in the triple sense of (1) the timing relevant to successful political campaigns, (2) the constrained or dark political times we feel ourselves to be in, and (3) appropriateness, mannerliness, or civility—timeliness as temperateness about when, how, and where one raises certain issues or mentions certain problems.[4] The first sense is concerned with strategy and efficiency in reaching a defined political end, the second speaks to holding back the dark, and the third invokes maturity and propriety against infantilism or indecorousness. Critique is taken to be at best irrelevant, at worst damaging, to the value represented by each.

The rebuff of critical theory as untimely provides the core matter of the affirmative case for it. Critical theory is essential in dark times not for the sake of sustaining utopian hopes, making flamboyant interventions, or staging irreverent protests, but rather to contest the very senses of time invoked to declare critique untimely. If the charge of untimeliness inevitably also fixes time, then disrupting this fixity is crucial to keeping the times from closing in on us. It is a way of reclaiming the present from the conservative hold on it that is borne by the charge of untimeliness.

To insist on the value of untimely political critique is not, then, to refuse the problem of time or timing in politics but rather to contest settled accounts of what time it is, what the times are, and what political tempo and temporality we should hew to in political life. Untimeliness deployed as an effective intellectual and political strategy, far from being a gesture of indifference to time, is a bid to reset time. Intellectual and political strategies of successful untimeliness therefore depend on a close engagement with time in every sense of the word. They are concerned with timing and tempo. They involve efforts to grasp the times by thinking against the times. They attempt, as Nietzsche put it, to "overcome the present" by puncturing the present's "overvaluation of itself,"[5] an overcoming whose aim is to breathe new possibility into the age. If our times are dark, what could be more important?

CRITICAL THEORY

To make the argument for critical theory as a hope rather than a luxury in dark times, we will need to think first a bit about critique, then about political time, and then about their relation.

Critique is an old term that derives from the Greek *krisis*. As the term flowered in modernity—and indeed, with Kant, came in part to define modernity—this connection between *krisis* and critique has been partly sustained, partly cast off. In ancient Athens, *krisis* was a jurisprudential term identified with the art of making distinctions, an art considered essential to judging and rectifying an alleged disorder in or of the democracy.[6] (In contrast to contemporary concerns with distinguishing the two, in its original usage critique is an explicit project of judgment.)[7] Since, in Athenian democracy, a defendant was also a citizen and Senate member, and the subset of the Senate constituting the jury also judged and sentenced the defendant, *krisis* referred to a scene in which the object, agent, process, and result of critique were intermingled. Procedurally, juridical *krisis* thus consisted of recognizing an objective crisis and convening subjective critics who then passed a critical judgment and provided a formula for restorative action.[8] Socratic critique converges with this practice in its dialectical and dialogical aspect, but breaks with it as it replaces an adjudicated truth with the search for a philosophical one. With the latter move, Socratic critique itself becomes a critique of the originally democratic and holistic form of *krisis*; embodied in the *Republic* and literalized in Socrates' defense at his trial (see Plato's *Apology*), the form, content, aim, and venue of Socratic philosophy is a critique of Athenian critique and, as such, of Athenian democracy.

The sifting and sorting entailed in Greek *krisis* focused on distinguishing the true from the false, the genuine from the spurious, the beautiful from the ugly, and the right from the wrong, distinctions that involved weighing pros and cons of particular arguments—that is, evaluating and eventually judging evidence, reasons, or reasoning.[9] *Krisis* thus comes close to what we would today call deliberation, and its connotations are quite remote from either negativity or scholasticism.[10] Since this practice also has a restorative aim in relation to the literal crisis provoking it, there could be no such thing as "mere critique," "indulgent critique," or even "untimely critique." Rather, the project of critique is to set the times right again by discerning and repairing a tear in justice through practices that are themselves exemplary of the justice that has been rent.

Again, this complex origin is evident in the way the project of philosophical critique takes shape for Socrates. Socratic critique was born of a monumental crisis, responding to the catastrophe of the Peloponnesian War, which resulted not simply in a lost empire but in a profoundly degraded, corrupted, and disoriented democracy. In this context, Socrates conceived the task of critique in keeping with the conceptual lines of the original *krisis*—to sort, sift, and set the times to rights—but as he made Athenian conceptions and practices of justice themselves the object of critique, he worked to remove from the hands of the demos the process of sorting and judging entailed in critique. Reconceived by Socrates as a philosophical activity both deriving from and producing individual virtue, even critique that involved discerning the nature of political justice was hived off from the political-juridical domain. This hiving off is explicitly expressed and defended in the *Apology* when Socrates explains his limited participation in Athenian political life by pointing out the impossibility of pursuing critique (and hence virtue) there. Thus critique loses its jurisprudential and political status and comes to be constituted as viable only at a certain remove from political life. Paradoxically, Socrates depicts critique both as inherently marginalized and neutered *by* politics if it refuses this remove, and yet as politically potent if it can ascertain the right degree of remove. Socrates responds to the collapse of Athenian holism, then, by ontologically separating the domains of politics and critical theory, at which point critical theory becomes (and has been ever after) a gadfly.

Etymologically, after antiquity, *criticism* and *critique* move apart from *crisis*, save for a certain sustained connection in the field of medicine, a usage that, according to Reinhart Kosseleck, developed in Latin in the Middle Ages to designate "the crucial stage of a disease in which a decision had to be made but had not yet been reached."[11] Crisis and criticism as a demand for judgment remain closely intertwined here, as indicated by the contemporary medical designation *critical condition*. Tellingly, we do not speak of the condition of someone mortally wounded or dying alone or among laypersons as "critical"; rather, this terminology is reserved for the dangerously ill within a medical facility or least in the presence of medical personnel, indicating that

accurate diagnosis and judgments about appropriate interventions potentially stand between life and death. This meaning lingers in political crisis as well. When we call a threshold moment in an international
standoff, in negotiations, or in a campaign "critical," we signal the
need for accurate assessment and effective strategies of action, all in a
context designated as urgent. A critical condition is thus a particular
kind of call: an urgent call for knowledge, deliberation, judgment, and
action to stave off catastrophe.

What is interesting in this contemporary trace of the old usage is the
sustained linking of the objective and subjective dimensions of critique, the ways in which a worldly event or phenomenon, whether a
collapsed empire or a diseased body, connects a specific condition with
an immediate need to comprehend by sifting, sorting, or separating its
elements, to judge, and to respond to it. Also noteworthy is the way
that critique is linked to temporal rupture and repair; critique as political *krisis* promises to restore continuity by repairing or renewing the
justice that gives an order the prospect of continuity, that indeed
makes it continuous.

This quality of urgency, this depiction of critique as nonoptional in
the restoration of an organism's or polity's health, continues through
Kant's account of the imperative of critique in establishing the moral
autonomy and hence freedom of the subject, and through Marx's turn
of this imperative to establishing the conditions for collective human
freedom. Attunement to this lineage provides a counterpoint to contemporary characterizations of critique as disinterested, distanced,
negating, or academic. It also counters the distinctly modern presumption of critique's dependency on and involvement with transcendent
Truth.[12]

POLITICAL TIME

This intentionally partial exercise in etymological memoration suggests certain ways in which the practice of critical theory inherently invokes a set of concerns with time. The crisis that incites critique and
that critique engages itself signals a rupture of temporal continuity,
which is at the same time a rupture in a political imaginary, a rupture
in a collective self-understanding dependent on the continuity of
certain practices. Or, as Derrida has taught us to read a line from
Shakespeare, for a polity suffering an internal crisis, where justice is

ruptured "the time is out of joint." Here is Derrida, riffing on the line from *Hamlet*: "'The time is out of joint': time is disarticulated, dislocated, dislodged, time is run down, on the run and run down, deranged, both out of order and mad. Time is off its hinges, time is off course, beside itself, disadjusted."[13] A polity in crisis is living out of its time, dissynchronic. In crisis, "the age is dishonored" consequent to what Derrida terms a rupture in *dike*'s conjoining power.[14] When a polity is in crisis, the times are unhinged, running off course; time itself lacks its capacity to contain us and conjoin us.

Critique's relation to crisis thus turns us toward the problem of political time, a time that is like no other time and incessantly morphs in meaning from tempo to temporality to periodicity to world condition, each sense implicated in every other. As with critique, it will be useful to juxtapose some formulations of specifically political time. Machiavelli figured political time as both beyond human control—the movement of events always has *Fortuna*'s hand in it—and as that element which every political virtuoso shapes to his own ends so as to triumph over Fortuna. While Fortuna signifies the extrahuman movement of political time, Machiavelli also conceived political time (and political space) as a wholly theatrical production, to be fashioned and fabricated as a political weapon. For Machiavelli, the construction of political time was importantly psychological in its effect, capable of producing different responses—panic, fear, boldness, lassitude—according to the seeming imminence or remoteness of a danger or possibility.[15]

William Connolly, drawing on Paul Virilio, emphasizes the phenomenon of speed as one of the most important features of late modernity. For Connolly, we are in the age of speed, which we had best catch up to if we are to be effective democrats.[16] Sheldon Wolin argues against such a catching up, indeed argues for a deliberate resistance on the part of radical democrats to the forced speedup of the political workplace. Wolin urges this resistance because political time, which he equates with democratic time, is necessarily *slow*, slower than anything else in late modern life: "It requires an element of leisure . . . in the sense . . . of a leisurely pace. This is owing to the needs of political action to be preceded by deliberation . . . . [P]olitical time is [also] conditioned by the presence of differences and the attempt to negotiate them."[17] Without the possibility of both deliberation and negotiation, and of the leisureliness that affords them, the conditions for democracy are literally eviscerated. This suggests that the political-as-the-democratic is terribly endangered in our time. Connolly regards Wolin's conclusion as an understandable but ultimately unacceptable nostalgia for a different (slower) age. If the tempo of late modernity is largely given by political economic and cultural forces, Connolly asks, hadn't we best locate or fashion democratic practices that can keep, or counter, the beat?[18]

Fredric Jameson diagnoses postmodernity as a condition in which "time consists in an eternal present and, much further away, an inevitable catastrophe, these two moments showing up distinctly on the registering apparatus without overlapping or transitional states. It is the next instant of time that falls out; we are like people only able to remember their distant pasts, who have lost the whole dimension of the recent and the most familiar."[19] The collapse of a sense of historical movement in the present betokens the loss of future possibility. This condition both occasions and allegorizes a collective paralysis that Jameson anguishes over. A present experienced as eternal is a present experienced as Total, with no imagined elsewhere. "It is a situation that endows the waiting with a kind of breathlessness, as we listen for the missing next tick of the clock, the absent first step of renewed praxis."[20]

The conference for which this essay was originally composed was titled "Critical Theory in Dark Times." It borrowed the phrase "dark times" from Hannah Arendt, and Arendt borrowed it from Brecht, and Brecht, I think, from the ancient Greeks. Such a chain of borrowings figures dark times as recurrent, thereby suggesting a certain genericism to the problem, just as the invocation of critical theory draws on a long historical vocation whose temporally local minions we would be. There have been dark times before—this is the significance of the plural noun, the reason why we speak of dark times rather than a dark time or a world cast into darkness. Indeed, there is something perversely hopeful in the appellation: dark times are episodic and finite, to be contrasted with an enduring condition or teleological trajectory. I wonder, though, if this hopefulness is self-certain, or perhaps instead counterphobic.

If this time of ours feels dark, in what does its darkness consist? I do not think we are talking simply about the difficulties of action or even about despair for the future in the face of unparalleled constellations of undemocratic power (neocolonial, capitalist, imperial, religious, terrorist) and of political visions dimmed by a century of failed alternatives. Rather, the reference would seem to conjure a child's experience of darkness, one rife with diabolical forces that can neither be mastered or comprehended, forces that frighten as they spook and heighten a felt impotence. The darkness signals not only danger but absence of illumination, and links the two: the dangers are greater because of the lack of light . . . or a good part of the danger inheres in the lack of light. We are disoriented, frightened, and stumbling in the dark.

There are two powers in our times whose main currency is fear: terrorism and empire. The principle of terrorism is unpredictable violence; it is the opposite of systematic, visible, routine, or regularized domination. What renders terrorist violence as power is its inevitable, anticipated, yet random arrival, its capacity to disrupt and destroy everyday life any time and any place. Because terrorism has no regular time or place, we are made fearful less by actual terrorist events than by the specter of terrorism, a specter that works through incalculability. This is the fundamental absurdity of color-coded "terror alerts." Feigning an ability to measure and predict the moves of a power form that mocks measurement and prediction, the alerts pretend in a way that convinces no one that we know what will happen next, that we are in control when we are not, even as they no doubt increase the fearfulness of those imagining themselves to be targets.

The principle of fear at work in contemporary practices of empire is quite different from that in terrorism and is related to the modern illegitimacy of empire vis-à-vis principles of democracy and popular sovereignty. This illegitimacy means that empire today can be justified only through fear, by declaring a perpetual state of emergency that would allow conventional democratic principles to be overridden. So modern empire mobilizes human fear on a mass scale; it is above all parasitic on the fear incited by the specter of terrorism, but it is also dependent on the fear related to the porousness of modern nation-states and to the exposure of vulnerable individuals and deracinated communities to the vicissitudes of global forces. Empire promises protection from dangers that it rhetorically magnifies in order to secure itself, a magnification that intensifies our fear in the dark.

But while darkness today implies not only fear but also disorientation, the latter pertains to an arc of powers shaping the present that exceed a dialectic of empire and terror. We are disoriented by the literal loss of trajectory following the collapse of historical metanarratives in a present that appears fraught with injustice and misery and not only apocalyptic danger. It has become a commonplace to describe our time as pounded by undemocratic historical forces yet lacking a *forward* movement. This makes the weight of the present very heavy: all mass, no velocity. Or, in the terms of the late modern speediness invoked earlier: all speed, no direction. If this heaviness mixed with speediness were analogized to a mental state, the diagnosis would be profound depressive anxiety, a disorder for which an astonishing number of persons today seek treatment. Depressive anxiety is a truly terrible state: you cannot move because of the bleakness but you cannot rest because of the anxiety; you can neither seize life nor escape it, neither live nor die. There may not be a better appellation for our condition, for the bleakness of a seemingly eternal present with catastrophe limning its horizon. Permanent daylight, Nietzsche reminds us, is one with unbroken darkness; the unbearability of both is time stopped, an endless present.[21] Unbroken time is the time of eternity, death's time. Little surprise, then, that we speak idiomatically of both time and darkness as "closing in on us." This quality of closure, this entrapment in an unbearable present, is a significant part of what makes our times dark today, what makes us unsure that it is just the times rather than the world that is darkening—indeed, what makes time and world collapse into one, because time, for all its speed, appears to have stopped going forward or taking us anywhere.

CRITICAL THEORY AND POLITICAL TIME

From Walter Benjamin, however, we know that there is fecundity and not only bleakness in the arrest of time. Benjamin regarded progressivism and historicism as the Scylla and Charybdis of critical thinking in dark times. For the journey through, he reconceived historical materialism as precisely that which stills time in the present and does so in order to make the present swerve, to knock it off course. Here is the sixteenth thesis of "Theses on the Philosophy of History":

> A historical materialist cannot do without the notion of a present which is not a transition, but in which time stands still and has come to a stop. For this notion defines the present in which he himself is writing history. Historicism gives the "eternal" image of the past; historical materialism supplies a unique experience with the past. The historical materialist leaves it to others to be drained by the whore called "Once upon a time" in historicism's bordello. He remains in control of his powers, man enough to blast open the continuum of history.[22]

In contrast with a conventional historical materialism that renders the present in terms of unfolding laws of history, Benjamin argues for the political and the philosophical value of conceiving the present as a time in which time is still(ed). But not only still—rather, it is a present in which time has come to a stop, thereby implying movement behind it. The affirmation of this temporal rush behind a still present, an affirmation that belies the stillness itself, avoids presentism and ahistoricity in political thinking even as it conceptually breaks the present out of history. But why does the historical materialist require this break? What is at stake in extracting this present from what Benjamin calls the "lifework" of history? Why this trick, and in what sense can we not do without it?

Benjamin's own answer: "this notion [of stillness] defines the present in which [the historical materialist] himself is writing history." Yes, this singular present impels and shapes the history being written, bringing Benjaminian historical materialism closer to genealogy as a past of the present, a past *for* the present, a history that has an aim with the present. But there is more at stake here than the self-consciousness of the theorist, and more too, than an empirical claim about how the living actually experience the present. Rather, an unmoving present, a present that is not automatically overcome by time, a present that is out of time in both senses, is a present that calls to us, calls on us to respond to it. Both the historical perspective and the political urgency of the critic are precipitated from this stillness—it contains the present's call. This is a call we will eventually want to articulate with the call, considered earlier, issued from a "critical condition."

The political stakes of the historical materialist, whom I am provisionally allowing to become one with the critical theorist, also appear in the next line of the thesis: "Historicism gives the 'eternal' image of the past; historical materialism supplies a unique experience with the past." Benjamin does not make the contrast of historicism with historical materialism turn simply on a particular method or conceptualization of history, though he does draw these distinctions (especially in the following thesis).[23] Rather, the present is the site of a particular *experience* of history, one in which the present is grasped as historically contoured but not itself experienced as history because not necessarily continuous with what has been. This experience of the present allows the historical materialist to render the present as ripe with non-utopian possibility—non-utopian because it is historically situated and constrained, a possibility because it is not historically foreordained or determined. Historical materialism renders the present historically yet *arrests* history for the present, and in that double gesture of power it becomes critical theory.[24]

In the final sentences of the thesis, the warring figures are manliness and whores: "The historical materialist leaves it to others to be drained by the whore called 'Once upon a time' in historicism's bordello. He remains in control of his powers, man enough to blast open the continuum of history." The trope of the whore who drains, who through her cheap yet seductive lure undermines man's will and strength, is no less misogynist because historicism itself is referred to as a bordello. The other of the whore is the virtuous wife and sublimated sexual energies, just as the other of the bordello is the procreative marital bed and sexual repression or regulation. Both recall the endless rehearsal in Western thought of manly autonomy undone by ungoverned female sexuality. The whorehouse figured not simply as moral corruption but as the scene of enervated masculine energies also figures woman controlled and subordinated (in marriage) as the precondition of manly public action. The whore that is historicism drains; the wife that is dialectical materialism leaves man in control of his powers to make the world.

If we were to paint this concern with action on a different lexical and literary landscape, however, we might examine without wincing Benjamin's aim to retrieve historical materialism both from the fatalistic "empty time" of the historicist and from the deterministic sigh of another conception of historical materialism. In insisting on the Nowness of the present as the impetus for the historical materialist, Benjamin depicts the historical materialist as rerouting by rethinking the work of history in the present, stilling time to open time. The possibility of "blasting open the continuum of history" with this rethinking literally makes the historical materialist, the critic, into dynamite.

There is a danger at this moment, of course, of conflating critical theory with political action, a conflation we will want to avoid.[25] But it is not clear that this is what Benjamin is arguing. Rather, he seems to be staging the present in terms of a constructed historical-political consciousness that itself blasts the present out of the continuum of history. A present figured as fecund rather than as determined on the one hand or as theologically presided over by empty time on the other produces what Benjamin famously calls "a revolutionary chance in the fight for the oppressed past."[26] Only a chance, but a revolutionary one: this struggle over what the past could mean in the present is at the same time a struggle for the future. Benjamin's meditation makes the project of critical theory into this reconfiguration of time in order to open the present, literally to let light into dark times.

THE TIME FOR CRITICAL THEORY

The art of engaged critical theory today involves attending to at least four related problematics of time, timeliness, and untimeliness: (1) knowing what time it is, a knowledge that includes (2) reckoning with the "out of jointness" of dark times, (3) thinking against the age or being untimely, and (4) shooting at the clocks, stilling or blowing up time in Benjamin's sense. To interweave these four problematics of time involves grasping the age historically, a comprehension that, with Nietzsche and Benjamin, sets it off from itself insofar as it breaks with the age's own self-conception, and at the same time tears the present out of a continuum of history. It also involves understanding untimeliness as the fruit of historical thinking, a genealogical plum that emerges not from an antihistorical stance but as a historical consciousness that works against an eternal present on the one hand and history as a run-on sentence on the other. Untimely critique that seeks to speak to our time is launched not from outside time, or indifferently to the times, but rather from historical materialism in control of its powers and wielded as a power. Thus Nietzsche's call for an "arrow shot into the age randomly and without guaranteed effect" is spurned by Sheldon Wolin's and Norman O. Brown's conviction that potent political critique must know what time it is—in short, must grasp the age.[27] Untimeliness is a technique for blowing up historical time, yet is only non-utopian to the extent that it exercises a profound reading of the times. If historical materialism aims to fracture a seamless present and to lift that present from seamless time, untimely critique insists on alternative possibilities and perspectives in a seemingly closed political and epistemological universe. It becomes a nonviolent mode of exploding the present.

The navigation of these four problematics of time might be conceived in terms of an *ethic* of timeliness and untimeliness in critical theory, one that involves both close attunement to the times and aggressive violation of their self-conception. This is by no means a comprehensive ethics but rather something like *an* ethic in Weber's sense—less a set of guidelines for action than a caution about what may not be discounted in acting.[28] (Weber's brief for "an ethic of responsibility" in politics has little positive content; it instead mainly consists of ruling out the disavowals entailed in other possible ethical stances.) An ethic of untimely critical theory, then, might consist in the following cautions.

On the one hand, critical theory cannot let itself be bound by political exigency; indeed, it has something of an obligation to refuse such exigency. While there are always decisive choices to be made in the political realm (whom to vote for, what policies to support or oppose, what action to take or defer), these very delimitations of choice are often themselves the material of critical theory. Here we might remind ourselves that prising apart immediate political constraints from intellectual ones is one path to being "governed a little less" in Foucault's sense. Yet allowing thinking its wildness beyond the immediate in order to reset the possibilities of the immediate is also how this degoverning rearticulates critical theory and politics after disarticulating them; critical theory comes back to politics offering a different sense of the times and a different sense of time. It is also important to remember that the "immediate choices" are just that and often last no longer than a political season (exemplified by the fact that the political conundrums with which this essay opened will be dated if not forgotten by the time this book is published). Nor is the argument convincing that critical theory threatens the possibility of holding back the political dark. It is difficult to name a single instance in which critical theory has killed off a progressive political project. Critical theory is not what makes progressive political projects fail; at worst it might give them bad conscience, at best it renews their imaginative reach and vigor.

On the other hand, critical theory concerned with politics is modestly bound not only to speak to the times but also to affirm them. In its historical-mindedness, critical theory is distinct both from normative moral theory, in its general refusal of historical specificity for its norms, and from utopian intellectual exercises, which attempt to leap out of history. But critical theory focused on political life is not negation, destruction, or nihilism; rather, critical theory aims to render crisis into knowledge, and to orient us in the darkness. Critique that does not affirm life, affirm value, and above all affirm possibilities in the present and the future, while certainly possible, is not making a bid for political power and hence cannot be understood as political. This does not mean that critiques must carry a full-blown political vision, declare "what is to be done," or advance transcendental or universal norms. But critical theory as political theory cannot get off the block without affirming contestable and contingent values, values that are themselves an affirmation of this world, and this time.

This final point can be put a little differently by returning to Foucault, with whom this essay begin. In "What Is Critique?" Foucault argues that historically, "critique is biblical," by which he means that for much of Western history not wanting to be governed "so much" or not wanting to be governed "like that" involved resisting church authority or scriptural prescription, in short, "refusing, challenging, limiting ecclesiastical rule." But this resistance, Foucault tells us, "meant returning to the Scriptures, seeking out what was authentic in them, what was really written in [them,] . . . questioning what sort of truth the Scriptures told."[29] Here we not only are recalled to the early meaning of critique as a process of sifting and distinguishing but are invited to understand critique as a practice of affirming the text it contests. Critique passionately reengages the text, rereads and reconsiders the text's truth claim. In so doing, critique reasserts the importance of the text under consideration (whether a law, nation, principle, practice, or treatise), its power to organize and contain us, its right to govern us. This affirmation of the text through an insistent rereading seems to me the heart of the distinction between critique and its cousins— rejection, refutation, rebuttal, dismissal. Critique, whether immanent, transcendent, genealogical, or in yet some other form, is always a rereading and as such a reaffirmation of that which it engages. It does not, it cannot, reject or demean its object. Rather, as an act of reclamation, critique takes over the object for a different project than that to which it is currently tethered. Critical theory in dark times thus affirms the times, renders them differently, reclaims them for something other than the darkness. In this sense, critical theory in dark times is a singular practice of *amor fati*.

T W O

■ ■ ■ ■

POLITICAL IDEALIZATION
AND ITS DISCONTENTS

Ritual recognizes the potency of disorder.
—MARY DOUGLAS, *Purity and Danger*

Everything that the [love] object does and asks for is right
and blameless[.]
—SIGMUND FREUD, *Group Psychology and the
Analysis of the Ego*

WHAT is political love and what is the relationship of political
love and political loyalty? If one loves a political community,
does such love require uncritical solidarity with certain elements of that community, and if so, with which elements—its laws, its
principles, its state institutions, its leaders, or actions taken in its
name? What kind of loyalty does political love engender and require,
to what extent is love compatible with critique, and to what extent is
critique compatible with loyalty? What counterintuitive compatibility
might be discerned between critique and fealty, between critique and
attachment, even between critique and love?

This essay explores these questions about civic or political love, fealty,
and critique through a consideration of the relationship of love and idealization. It considers this relationship as it emerges both in conservative
expressions of national patriotism and in radical dissent from state policy. It asks about the productivity as well as the costs of political idealization, and considers how we might successfully navigate some of its
perils as we think about, and practice, democratic citizenship.

These reflections were incited by the widespread call for American national unity in the immediate aftermath of 9/11. For the most part, this call demanded unwavering patriotism, uncritical support for policies formulated by the Bush administration, and solidarity with a national narrative about our goodness and our victimhood. In this context, criticism of America or dissent from state policy were, quite simply, equated with disloyalty. And disloyalty, in turn, associated dissenters with what, overnight, had become the enemy.

The equation of dissent with disloyalty has its cultural and political ramifications, especially when combined with state declarations such as "if you're not with us, you're against us," a formulation that tacitly endorses restrictions on dissent enacted by corporate and media powers while sustaining the legitimacy of the state as a protector of free speech.[1] However, the most worrisome ramifications may be less the explicit incidents of censorship than the discursive framing of all dissent as un-American, a framing that not only constrains what may be said *and* heard, but replaces a critically important political debate about what America is, stands for, or ought to do in world politics with a more polemical argument about loyalty or a more narrowly legalistic one about free speech. The instantiation of this polemicism and this legalism in the title and substance of the USA Patriot Acts, and in the now unquestionably necessary arguments about those pieces of legislation, is but one example of this diversion.

Two caveats before beginning. What follows is not intended as universal formulation of the relationship between citizenship, loyalty, and critique; rather, it explores these relations as they are configured by a time of crisis and by a liberal democratic state response to that crisis. The essay does not ask, generically, whether there is some point at which political dissent or critique undercuts citizenship or some point at which political rebellion is legitimate. Rather, it considers the relation of love, loyalty, and critique within a political order, the existence and basic legitimacy of which is not called into question.[2] In other words, this is a distinctly nonrevolutionary formulation of the problematic of dissent; it not only presumes something of a stable nation-state population but presumes as well an investment from both critics and noncritics in preserving rather than overthrowing the state.

A second caveat concerns the effect on nation-state citizenship of the dramatic transnational migrations occasioned by the latest phase of capital, often termed globalization. My argument presumes reasonably strong identification by citizens with the nation-states in which they are living. However, this identification cannot be taken for granted today. Western liberal democracies harbor substantial and growing populations that often have limited identification with and fealty toward the states they find themselves living in, or that may have fealty in the direction of two or more "nations," or that may assert a cosmopolitan "world citizenship" or "transnational citizenship" rather than one tied to a single nation-state. Apart from the question of immigration occasioned by globalization, nation-states themselves are receding, however slowly and unevenly, as the basis of collective identification and collective action. It may be that nothing is so important as trying to understand what nation-state citizenship—loyal, critical, disgruntled, or otherwise—means in this historical context, but that is not the aim of this essay.

SOCRATIC LOYALTY

We begin with Socrates and the complex model of radical patriotism that is figured in the Platonic dialogues concerned with his trial and death sentence. Socrates, who insisted on the intimacy of love and citizenship, love and knowledge, love and virtue. Socrates, who embodied a perverse but compelling form of citizenship rooted in challenging the premises and practices of the status quo, indeed, who made intellectual work into a distinct form of citizenship. Socrates, who would not flee the city that voted to execute him for his peculiar way of loving it, but also would not be bullied into a more conventional form of affection. Surely this character is almost too extreme for thinking about today's dissident—rarely intellectual, often angry and alienated from other citizens, hardly a practitioner of love, and more likely to sue the state for abridged liberties than to bow before its sentencing. Yet, as the etymology of *theory* itself recalls—in ancient Greece, *theōria* emerged as a term for seeing enriched by journeying—there is often self-knowledge buried in places remote from our own.

In the *Apology* and the *Crito*, Socrates wrestles with the nature of his relationship and obligations to Athens, both of which configure his life as philosopher and critic, and both of which are activated as topics by his conviction and sentencing. Charged with corrupting the youth and with a specific kind of impiety—introducing new divinities—Socrates understands these charges to be rooted in the effects of his vocational calling and especially in the effects of his relentless critical interrogation of the contemporary Athenian way of life. In his defense against the charges, Socrates literally reverses them, casting his practice of questioning every individual and collective practice in Athens as a supreme act of loyalty not simply to an inner calling or to truth but to Athens itself. He roots this claim of loyalty in his love for the citizens of Athens, a love practiced and demonstrated by his commitment to improving them, a commitment for which he stakes his life. Pressing the argument still further, Socrates insists that he cares far more about Athenian citizens than his accusers do, indeed cares about them so much that he is willing to be put to death for his efforts on their behalf, just as devoted soldiers are willing to die in battle:

> For wherever a man's place is, whether the place which he has chosen or that in which has been placed by a commander, there he ought to remain in the hour of danger, taking no account of death or of anything else in comparison with disgrace. . . . Strange, indeed, would be my conduct, O men of Athens, if I who, when I was ordered by the generals whom you chose to command me at Potidaea and Amphipolis and Delium, remained where they placed me, like any other man, facing death—if now, when, as I conceive and imagine, God orders me to fulfill the philosopher's mission of searching into myself and other men, I were to desert my post through fear of death. (*Apology* 28d–e)[3]

The comparison with military service is no minor one, of course, since the soldier in battle is the ultimate icon of civic loyalty and it is Socrates' loyalty to Athens that is at issue. Yet the comparison could also not be more strained: the city's generals command the soldier while "God" commands Socrates, and the question of which god(s) Socrates hears or obeys—an Athenian god or a "foreign" one— animates one of the main questions about his potential civic subversiveness. Indeed, the tension between the fealty Socrates may have to a god other than Athens or to other than an Athenian god is articulated by this comparison even as it is also rhetorically finessed by it. If Socrates' daemon is uniquely his and if the God commanding him is Truth rather than an Athenian deity, then even his willingness to die for his commitment sustains rather than eradicates the potential tension between his inner calling and his civic loyalty, between serving truth and the effect of this service on the city he claims to love. Socrates finesses the tension through the trope of sacrifice and through the figure of the servant common to both, and thus allows obedience as such—to the point of risking death—to constitute proof of his loyal character. But civic patriotism is not loyalty as such and is not measured by willingness to die for one's cause whatever it is; rather it entails loyalty to the specific collectivity by which one is harbored and is generally measured by willingness to sacrifice for that collectivity.

Still, in this articulation and finesse, Socrates has articulated a dimension of our problem for us: Is political fealty appropriately attached to actually existing political communities, to their laws, policies or utterances, or to the political ideals we hold out for these communities? Is it sometimes one and sometimes the other? How to know which, when? If one loves another Athens, another America than the one whose actions or laws we decry in the present, what is the place of loyalty in mediating between this love and the polity as it presents itself now, here? Or, if one loves what one is harbored by but is also ruthlessly critical of and devoted to trying to improve, is this loyalty? When might thoughtful disagreement or passionate critique be the ultimate act of love, even the ultimate act of solidarity—not simply because it is engaged but because it constitutes a more comprehensive address of this attachment insofar as it engages the ambivalence inherent in passionate attachment?

From Socrates in the *Apology*, we have an argument that dissent from existing practices, even wholesale critique of the regime, is not merely compatible with love and loyalty to a political community, but rather is the supreme form of such love and loyalty. Moreover, it would seem that dissent can have this value even when it happens at the fringes of the regime, outside the domain of the officially political realm and thus outside the usual purview of citizenship, suggesting that it need not be a critique with immediate political efficacy where the political is equated with policy. Socrates makes the case for intellectual critique as the highest form of loyalty if and when this critique is aimed at improving the *virtue* of the citizens.

In arguing that his unconventional ways and venue of working permit the greatest expression of political loyalty to the city, Socrates implies that the conventional political and military domains are not so fertile for the practice of loyalty understood as love—they are too fraught with immediate concerns of the day, with power politics, and above all, too inimical to the thoughtfulness that he takes as both the basis and the necessary content of this love; dutiful citizens carrying out an unjust policy or dutiful soldiers fighting an unjust war are presumably slavish and unthinking rather than loving in their loyalty.[4] What is also striking about Socrates' argument is that even as it is couched in terms compatible with modern Thoreauvian themes of individual conscience, he is making not a moral or ethical argument but rather a political one about what constitutes true citizenship and loyalty. Nor is this reducible to a claim that "the examined life" is the most valuable thing for the polis. Instead, it is an argument that citizenship consists of a relation to individual virtue, to justice, and thus, a relation of citizen to citizen rather than simply a relationship of citizen to state. Indeed, it is a casting of citizenship itself as a cultivation of virtue in oneself and others rather than as an orientation toward law and the state.

Dana Villa's recent work, *Socratic Citizenship*, allows us to take this point further and to connect it with the problematic of critique. Villa argues that the Socratic activity of disputing common opinion—of what Villa calls "dissolving and purging"—would be mistakenly construed as only a project of disillusionment. Rather, drawing on Arendt, Villa argues that Socrates' commitment to thinking, and to inciting thoughtfulness in his fellow citizens, is a strategy for averting evil and injustice. In Arendt's study of Eichmann, she argued that the precondition for radical political evil is not some moral or ontological predisposition to evil but rather "ingrained thoughtlessness," and it is precisely such routine thoughtlessness that Socrates aims to disrupt.[5] If citizen virtue consists in avoiding evil, and evil springs from such thoughtlessness, then thinking itself becomes the ultimate citizen virtue. Two conclusions follow from this positing of an inherent relation between thoughtfulness and justice, and between justice and citizenship. First, any moral or political belief that is sheltered from interrogation, insofar as it becomes a thoughtlessly held belief, becomes an incitement to injustice.[6] Second, insofar as Socratic thoughtfulness—the work of interrogation and critique—requires a certain withdrawal from the immediate scene of political life, part of the action of political justice inherently occurs in a distinctly nonpolitical realm, in what Socrates called private life but in what we would call intellectual (not necessarily academic) life, impossibly fully public but also not private in the modern sense. As Villa concludes, the kind of thinking Socrates requires to avert evil and cultivate virtue, to be a good citizen, cannot take place in the public realm.[7]

In sum, Socrates' defense in the *Apology* would seem to make an argument for (1) critique as the basis for practicing virtue and justice, and hence as essential rather than inimical to civic loyalty;[8] (2) the space of this critique as one that either redefines the parameters of the political to include this intellectual work, this cultivation of thoughtfulness apart from the public realm, or alternatively, puts political life into necessary tension with intellectual life; (3) love of one's fellow citizens as the index of civic loyalty; and (4) devotion to improving citizen virtue as the index of this love. Again, this defense should not be misread as cultivating merely private virtue, merely individual dissent to the existing state, or merely intellectual critique of political life. Rather, Socrates aims to render politically potent a space (the private), an activity (philosophizing, critique), and relations (of individual citizens to one another and of the intellectual to the political) ordinarily conceived as unpolitical or irrelevant to the political. Perversely, his trial and punishment suggest at least partial success in this aim; the philosophical "gadfly" was figured by his accusers as a consequential political player in Athens.

But within the framework of political loyalty I have been developing via Socrates, what are the limits to critique and, in particular, where might these limits obtain political definition? How far can critique go, and in particular how aggressive can it be toward the polity before it ceases to be loyal where loyalty is defined as love? What must be preserved or protected amid its deconstructive aims? The dialogue *Crito* offers something of an answer to these questions; the dialogue sketches a political container for the work of critique in the form of a warning against excessively loosening the threads of the collectivity that sustain its inhabitants. Indeed, the dialogue as a whole represents a kind of limit on the activities defended in the *Apology*, a limit in which Socrates' own preference for living in the city of Athens is made to represent a tacit commitment not to violate or destroy the collectivity that has harbored, educated, and sustained him. The dialogue also argues that the work of critique, Socrates' work, must be preservative, and to this end must be animated by love, or else it will neither carry its own limits nor have any reason to be tolerated by those who wish to preserve the state. Socrates, in other words, was not a simple defender of political free speech nor a detractor of it. Rather, he was concerned with the kinds of critical speech that are politically and ethically valuable and legitimate.

The dialogue begins with Socrates' corrupt old friend, Crito, coming to Socrates' prison on the morning he is to be executed. Crito's aim is to persuade Socrates to escape prison and flee Athens. Crito knows it is useless to ask Socrates to do this out of his own self-interest, so he appeals to Socrates' sense of friendship: "people who do not know you and me will believe that I might have saved you if I had been willing to spend money, but that I did not care" (*Crito* 44c). This concern gives Socrates a final chance to respond to his accusers: he argues that the opinion of the many is unimportant compared to living virtuously, indeed that concern with the opinion of the many is at odds with living honorably (*Crito* 47–48). But then Socrates turns to the question of the proposed escape itself, asking not simply whether it would be acceptable to escape but whether it would serve virtue and justice to do so. For Socrates, this question ceases to be one concerned either with the character of his accusers or with his alleged crimes, and turns instead upon the nature of his belonging to Athens, and more specifically upon whether he may break the laws of Athens to preserve his own life.

Now, given Socrates' declared object of political attachment in the *Apology*, namely the citizenry, why this sudden concern with the laws as an object and measure of political fealty? What force or authority are the laws being made to carry here? And in the question of what constitutes his political obligation, why focus on laws rather than principles or practices—Socrates' usual focus in thinking about virtue? Why is an obligation to God, to truth, to wisdom, to philosophy, and to virtue not more compelling than an obligation to the laws he has spent his life interrogating and criticizing, at times even belittling? And why this stubborn refusal to acknowledge that, in his own case, the laws have been, in Foucault's parlance, "used as tactics,"[9] and that in honoring the decision wrought from them, their tactical and corrupt deployment is dissimulated again?

Why the laws? Socrates lets the laws themselves answer this question, which of course they do with great partiality to their case. They tell him first that the proposed act of escape is one which brings the state to ruin: "Do you imagine that a state can subsist and not be overthrown, in which the decisions of law have no power, but are set aside, and trampled upon by individuals?" (*Crito* 50b). They argue, second, that they are his true parents, "more precious and higher and holier far than mother or father or any ancestor," and that as such, he has no right to destroy them, even as they may have him destroyed (*Crito* 50e, 51a). So Socrates is enjoined from doing anything that (a) ruins the state, and (b) violates, degrades, or defies what has given him life, indeed, what has given him his life work, what has made him Socrates. But is Socrates really arguing that the laws are the soul and sinew of the state? If so, what is the difference between disobeying the law (as he did, for example, when he would not fetch Leon from Salamis) and refusing to submit to the law's punishment for disobeying it? Why is one kind of civil disobedience less harmful to the state than another? And what distinction does Socrates allow between the laws themselves and their interpretation and use by men? To which is one obliged? What is the significance, too, of this homage to the laws and the state from one who has just insisted upon the impossibility of knowing and pursuing virtue in public life, and has argued instead for the supervening value of tending individual souls, from one who has essentially argued against the potential for virtue in the political domain, a domain of which the laws are a part? Finally, in what sense are the laws "parents" and what is the significance of this discourse for thinking about Socratic dissent?

I want to suggest that *Crito* should not be treated as a literal defense of the laws as an object of unconditional fealty. Rather, read alongside the *Apology*, *Crito* argues for honoring—or better, preserving—whatever stands for the integrity of the collectivity, what binds and regenerates the collectivity over time. In the *Apology*, Socrates argued that intellectual life, and especially its cultivation of thoughtfulness, was utterly crucial in this regard. If the laws are also crucial, it is not because they are authoritative or because they are rules but because they generate and sustain the collectivity. When they say to Socrates, "we have brought you into the world and reared you and educated you," they are describing this generativity and posing the question of what it would mean to injure or demean it; they are reminding Socrates of his own constitution by the polis he has criticized and are thereby delineating a crucial distinction between political critique and political destruction (*Crito* 51c).[10] Indeed, figured as parents, and speaking to him remonstratively, the laws recall the deep attachment, the love, that constitutes the ground and the urgency of Socratic criticism, configuring it as a force for improvement or transformation rather than destruction, and establishing its limit at the place where the one veers into the other. The laws frame Socrates' work—they permit it (by permitting freedom of speech), they may well incite it (by being unjust or impoverished, or simply by provoking reflection about the justice they are meant to represent), but they also contain it as they contain him, indeed as they *possess* him by virtue of their care for him.

Another way to see this: the laws as Socrates has figured them in *Crito* are simultaneously dialogic and authoritative, intellectual and paternal. That is, on the one hand, they speak as Socrates ordinarily speaks; they become Socratic, and interrogate Socrates as if he were one of the slightly dim-witted interlocutors he so often contends with, posing questions whose answers are largely given in the question and patiently leading Socrates to an inexorable and incontestable conclusion. But in assuming this dialogic character, they do not appear as static or formulaic things to be obeyed; rather they embody the very thoughtfulness and capacity for instruction and improvement that Socrates wants to place at the heart of the polis, that Socrates insists is the essence of justice. "[A]ll our orders," they declare, "are in the form of proposals, not of savage commands, and we give him the choice of either persuading us or doing what we say" (*Crito* 51e). In part, then, it is this instructive, even philosophical quality of the laws that Socrates wants to protect and preserve. However, on the other hand, in the move to personify the laws as all-powerful parents—both generative of life and capable of taking it away—Socrates has also defined a locus of political authority that is not purely dialogic and certainly not a fount of freedom or egalitarianism. The laws describe Socrates as their "child and servant" and ask: "do you imagine that what is right for us is equally right for you, and that whatever we try to do to you, you are justified in retaliating? You did not have equality of rights with your father or your employer . . . ; you were not allowed to answer back when you were scolded or to hit back when you were beaten . . . . Do you expect to have such license against your country and its laws that if we try to put you to death in the belief that it is right to do so, you on your part will try your hardest to destroy your country and us its laws in return?" (*Crito* 50e).

So there is both authority and philosophical wisdom at the core of the laws' claim on Socrates; but in casting this combination in the figure of the father, Socrates has also gestured toward the idealization of the state so essential to its binding function as a state as well as generative of our loyalty to it. That is, in letting the authority of the laws stand for the state, in idealizing this authority as both powerful and wise (and yet also as vulnerable to injury), and in personifying this authority as parental, Socrates has recalled the libidinal and emotional investments that citizens must have in the insignias of the collectivity for the collectivity to bind a people together and command its fealty. At the same time, in personifying the laws as parents, Socrates has landed us on rich psychoanalytic terrain where parents are not just what one loves or reveres but also what one hates and wants to kill, what one desires either to have or to be, what one wants to triumph over or destroy, what one wants to be loved by and for whose love one rivals one's siblings, what one has eternal longing, aggression, and guilt toward. It is nearly impossible, then, to regard this metaphor as innocent or to ignore the rich cauldron of feeling toward the polity and the state that it signals.

FREUDIAN CIVIC BONDS

In taking up the challenge to think psychoanalytically about the state-citizen relation, I will not consider all that is entailed in formulating this relation in terms of the filial psyche but rather will focus upon the place of *idealization* and *identification* in generating political fealty and conditioning the specific problematic of dissent amid this fealty. In particular, I want to consider the ways that the extreme idealization of the state required for loyalty binds or suppresses an inherent hostility toward the idealized object, a hostility that dissent or critique may articulate. But not only articulates; rather, these isolated and episodic bouts of dissent or critique have the potential to incite a generalized desublimation of the repressed hostility in idealization—what Freud calls the "contagion effect" of violated taboos—thereby imperiling the consolidating power of the idealization. It is because it carries this potential that domestic dissent appears and is cast (by the state, by patriotic citizens) as allied with attacks from outside—each exposes the vulnerability of the nation and what binds it, each de-idealizes albeit in a different way (one by challenging the good of the nation, the other by challenging its strength). The challenge, then, is to discern how critique can be fashioned as a productive de-idealization, one that features and preserves the love that incites or generates it. This challenge would require reorientation on the part of both the critic/dissident and the patriot, the combined figure of which might be said to be Socrates, to whom we will therefore eventually return.

From Freud, we learn that all love requires idealization and that idealization itself is a complex combination of narcissistic projection and sexual inhibition—the latter because love is already an inhibition of a more primary aim, sexual desire.[11] The mechanics of idealization are such that "the object is . . . treated in the same way as our own ego, so that when we are in love a considerable amount of narcissistic libido overflows on to the object" (*GP*, 112). In many cases, Freud argues, the love object is a substitute for some unattained ego ideal of our own—"We love it on account of the perfections which we have striven to reach for our own ego, and which we should now like to procure in this roundabout way as a means of satisfying our own narcissism" (*GP*, 113). For Freud, then, there is no such thing as simply loving another for intrinsically worthy qualities or capacities; the lover is always recasting the beloved according to her or his own ideals and ego needs. The lover is also always busily suppressing hostilities toward the love object in order to love, *and* is always navigating between a desire to have and to be the love object. Idealization, which at its extreme refuses to countenance the perception of any flaws or limitations in the love object, assists in all of these projects, and this especially with love that is not sexually gratified. (Sexual gratification, Freud reminds us, must inherently reduce the idealization or "overvaluation" that love entails—since love springs from repression of the sexual impulse.) Here is how Freud depicts this extreme idealization:

> Contemporaneously with this "devotion" of the ego to the object, which is no longer to be distinguished from a sublimated devotion to an abstract idea, the functions allotted to the ego ideal entirely cease to operate. The criticism exercised by that agency is silent; everything that the object does and asks for is right and blameless. Conscience has no application to anything that is done for the sake of the object; in the blindness of love remorselessness is carried to the pitch of crime. The whole situation can be completely summarized in a formula: *The object has been put in the place of the ego ideal.* (*GP*, 113)

Love is devotion to an abstract idea projected onto an object, but this devotion relieves the lover's superego of its ordinary tasks—that superego has been supplanted by the projections onto the love object. Thus, the lover is not only uncritically enthralled, without any capacity to judge or criticize the object, but also potentially criminal in this enthrallment—without any capacities of conscience to limit what she or he will do for the beloved or in the name of love. Although we are not quite ready to make the homological move to love of country, it is worth noting how this account resonates with a conventional kind of patriotic zeal. The patriot idealizes the country which is indistinguishable from an abstract idea (e.g., of what America stands for) and devotes him- or herself to this ideal. The country is all, the patriot nothing, except in his or her devotion. There is no limit on what the country can ask for nor on what the patriot will do for the country, including violent, criminal, or suicidal acts.

To this point, we have considered idealization in love as an individual matter; but since we are trying to learn something about the ways of civic love, love that is oriented toward the state and embraces the collectivity that the state interpellates, we need to supplement this account with considerations of the dynamics peculiar to group idealizations. In *Totem and Taboo* and *Group Psychology and Analysis of the Ego*, Freud offers an analysis of the distinctive ways that love's complexities operate for groups, and more precisely, of how the reproduction of an ideal binds the group and in particular contains its ambivalence about its love object. In contrast with other moral and clinical psychologists of his day, most notably Le Bon, Freud does not think that group and individual psychology stem from different parts of the psyche or involve different impulses; rather, for Freud, group psychology is an aspect of individual psychology, not a distinctive psychological form (*GP*, 69–70). This is so because Freud does not take human beings to be group animals but rather, inherently socially rivalrous and competitive, a feature born from sibling jealousies over parental love. Thus, Freud's challenge is to decipher what generates and then binds a group, how individual psyches repress, divert, or sublimate this natural rivalry. Freud's answer is simultaneously simple and complex: groups are constituted by shared love for something or someone that is outside the group and even at some distance from the group. "Originally rivals, [individuals] . . . succeed . . . in identifying themselves with one another by means of a similar love for the same object" (*GP*, 120). *Homo sapiens*, Freud argues, is not a herd animal but a horde animal, "an individual creature in a horde led by a chief" (*GP*, 121).

A group becomes possible, then, when individuals put one and the same object in place of their ego ideal and consequently *identify themselves with one another in their ego*. Where for Hobbes, it is *fear* that gathers us, for Freud it is love; we are bound to one another through our collective experience of being in love with something that none of us can have, a bond that itself sustains the love and even gives the love a field of expression that the remoteness of the object would otherwise deny.[12] The group confirms the love and gives it a reality unavailable to the lone individual beholden to a remote object. (It is the sight of American flags everywhere, and not just his or her own, that gladdens the heart of the patriot.) In short, a group is achieved through identification in love, and is threatened by the sundering of that identification or the collapse of that love.

So, the difference between individual love and group formation is that in the latter, individuals replace their natural rivalry toward one another with identification, an identification achieved by loving the same object. And when this love is not attached explicitly to a person ("a chief"), it will be to something else iconic of the group (e.g., the image of the nation, or the power of the nation), something outside that binds the inside. However, the attachment, given the nature of the displacement and identification it issues from, produces two very significant, indeed troubling effects for democratic citizenship even as it binds citizens into a nation: first, the attachment achieved through idealization is likely to glory in the *power* of the nation, a power expressed in state action; second and relatedly, because individual ego ideals have been displaced onto the nation, citizenship and patriotism are rendered as both passive and uncritical adoration of this power. Power thus replaces democracy as the love object, and passivity, obeisance, and uncritical fealty replace active citizenship as the expression of love. In this way, the psychoanalytic roots of nationalism appear as directly antidemocratic to the extent that the latter is understood as the sharing of power and the deliberation and thoughtfulness this sharing requires.

Moreover, this kind of love depends upon sustaining a very high level of idealization to counter the hostility that all feelings of love involve, and it depends as well upon externalizing this hostility. As Freud puts the matter in *Civilization and Its Discontents*, "it is always possible to bind together a considerable number of people in love, so long as there are other people left over to receive the manifestation of their aggressiveness."[13] The development of group cohesion thus depends upon turning aggression and hostility outward; maintenance of this cohesion depends upon keeping that aggression externalized; group narcissism allows the group to do this guiltlessly and even across potentially divisive stratifications within the group.[14] Still there is a precariousness to this achievement. First, in Freud's account, high levels of idealization, and particularly expressions of unqualified adoration and devotion, are themselves often signs of the unconscious hostility inherent in love. As he argues in *Totem and Taboo*, solicitous "over-affection," e.g., of a young child for a mother, or between members of a married couple, is a way of "shouting down" this hostility and therefore also an obvious sign of its presence.[15] So the lover finds her- or himself in a condition in which she or he must refuse all evidence of flaws in the object, shout down her or his own aggression toward the object, and denounce others' aggression toward the object. This condition compounds the tendency, already identified above in the psychodynamics of nationalism, toward a radical rejection of what we have identified as Socratic thoughtfulness, both in oneself or others; indeed, this condition will necessarily equate thoughtfulness with potential danger to the idealization and hence to the polity. It is inherently anti-intellectual. It is also a condition that would appear to entail lots of shouting.

The replacement of rivalry with identification through group love for the same object is precarious, secondly, because of what Freud formulates as anxiety about the contagion effect of taboo violation—a violation that breaks the collective awe of the taboo and especially the commitment to repressing hostility toward the revered object or being that is represented by the taboo. In Freud's account, the fear is that if one person succeeds in gratifying a repressed or unconscious desire, and that gratification is not immediately punished or avenged by the group, the same desire is bound to be kindled in other members of the community (*TT*, 71). To avert this contagion in the context of a relatively free social order, there must be a relatively even suppression of ambivalence toward the collective love object among members of a group. That is, the level of collective idealization must be pitched high and must be internally policed, even if this policing is not legally sanctioned or institutionally enforced. This is the basic structure of conventional patriotism's intolerance of critique.

We are now in a position to understand something of how the internal criticism of a nation, for those who have invested their uncritical love there, does not simply entail the wound of having one's love object faulted but rather appears to threaten the very bonds of the nation by challenging both the identification and the idealization constituting these bonds. Moreover, such criticism effectively gives voice to the hostility suppressed by undying devotion; and once voiced, this hostility is potentially contagious, again threatening both the identification and the idealization that binds the nation. Finally, to the extent that such criticism does figure a certain unleashing of aggression toward the nation, it represents the desublimation of aggression in group love that is ordinarily turned outward toward what is named as an enemy. That is, if groups achieve harmony within by diverting aggression outward, not only toward that which does not share their love but toward that which is imagined as opposite to their love—figured as the Other of their idealized object—criticism brings the aggression back inside, which again threatens the identification as well as the idealization binding the nation.

This aggression turned inward, of course, can be turned again, by the patriots or the state, against the dissenter. Nothing does this more effectively than the discursive mechanism of linking domestic dissent with the enemy, correlating internal critique or de-idealization with external attack—"if you're not with us, you're against us." But this is not a purely tactical move. Both external attack and internal dissent wound the narcissism of the lover by challenging the idealization, especially if that idealization fetishizes strength or invulnerability and not simply goodness. Both threaten the group with disintegration, both reveal the thinness of the membrane binding the nation. It is hardly surprising, then, that they would appear not merely equivalent but collusive, leading the zealous patriot to denounce the dissenter as a traitor—"giving aid and comfort to the enemy."

Briefly now I want to make a turn from Freud to Slavoj Žižek in order to plot one more line in this picture, one that will deepen our understanding of the peculiar character of identification involved in a certain kind of patriotism, and one that will allow us to see why dissent is problematic not only for maintaining idealization in general, but for maintaining the kind of identification upon which a liberal democratic patriotic ideal depends. In *The Sublime Object of Ideology*, Žižek theorizes political idealization as dependent not merely upon imaginary but symbolic identification. Whereas imaginary identification is identification with the *objects in* an image, symbolic identification involves identification with the gaze that produces the image, and thus is not only socially located elsewhere from the depicted objects, but may be animated and organized by very different desires and social forces. In Žižek's own words, "imaginary identification is identification with the image in which we appear likeable to ourselves, with the image representing 'what we would like to be,' and symbolic identification, identification with the very place *from where* we are being observed, *from where* we look at ourselves so that we appear to ourselves likeable, worthy of love."[16] So, for example, in an image of America as good, free, and true, but injured by evildoers who "hate our way of life," imaginary identification involves identifying with wounded goodness, while symbolic identification identifies with the power that generates this image, "the place from which such 'good' images are seen . . . the place of those who need to legitimize their domination and exploitation of others, those who disguise their aggressivity through the active invocation of a positive image that becomes . . . the symptom, the excess, the secret enjoyment of their lives."[17] If imaginary identification tends toward identification with powerlessness in such scenes, symbolic identification identifies with power, but dissimulates this identification in the image of purity or woundedness through which it is achieved.

In her discussion of Žižek, Rey Chow notes that the significance of symbolic identification is often neglected (in intellectual and political life) precisely because it does not rely upon resemblance.[18] Thus, not just ordinary discourse but theoretical discourse tends to treat idealizations rather literally, that is, as a literal idealization of a loved object—whether an individual, a polity, a class or group—and fails to ask the question: "for whom is the subject enacting this role? Which gaze is considered when the subject identifies himself with a certain image?"[19] That is, even when citizens are identifying with images, say, of an innocent and well-meaning people, this imaginary identification is performed for an observing gaze, potentially internal but mirroring the external one of the powerful imperial state. The imaginary and symbolic identifications are thus made simultaneously and in relationship to one another.

The idealizations that symbolic identification generates and lives off of are extremely powerful as legitimation strategies; the work of symbolic identification here is to generate a patriotic ideal that disavows its imbrication with state violence, imperial arrogance, aggression toward outsiders. In Rey Chow's account, the point of language which "proclaims/presents a noble idea/image of 'the people'" is "to seduce—to divert attention away from the rulers' violence and aggressivity at the same time that sympathy/empathy with the good idea/image is aroused."[20] The image of a free and good people conjured by contemporary patriotic idealizations generates sympathy, especially if such a people have suffered a wound; but this sympathy, indeed, this idealization, masks the symbolic identificatory function which it also generates—identification with the power that can generate such an image in the first place, that is outside the wound, that delivers the wound, that may be non-innocent, powerful, ignoble, imperial, and/or abusive.[21] Identification with power, which is what I am suggesting "my country is always right" patriotism entails, calls for loyalty to power rather than principle; it glories not in the goodness of America but in its power; it needs other nations and peoples to defer to this power and suffers a narcissistic wound when they do not. This is a dangerous political condition, not only because of the volatility and aggression in this kind of patriotism, but because it breeds anti-intellectualism, contempt for thoughtfulness and collective introspection, and disdain for peacemaking. Certainly the wrath turned against any attempt, in the autumn of 2001, at understanding how America contributed to its own making as a target of Third World and specifically Arab rage is a symptom of this condition. Indeed, the extent to which the plaintive and victimized refrain "why do they hate us so?" was accompanied by a relentless refusal to entertain plausible answers to the question exemplifies the double operation of imaginary and symbolic identification in patriotic idealizations of America. The question invokes the image of aggression against our innocence and goodness and invites identification with the victimized innocents; the refusal identifies with the arrogance of state power and supremacy that feels no need to know anything about its place in the world or to know much of anything about the rest of the world.

Žižek's distinction between imaginary and symbolic identification allows us to understand the extent to which a seemingly benign patriotic identification, one based in a celebration of the "American way of life," may disguise its own love of state power, its own enthrallment to the power of the father, and its own potential feasting upon state violence. The patriotism formally features the goodness of the regime and the fineness of the people, not the power of the father to give or take away life, not what Socrates, in openly describing the paternal nature of the state and the filial nature of his obligation or fealty, expressed more directly—that it is in relation to the state's *power* that he curtails his defiance of the state and becomes deferential. This curtailment arises not from intimidation by state power but because he responds libidinally to this aspect of the state, because he idealizes the state as the father, and idealizes the father as a literally boundless object of devotion and love. This is the idealization that binds Socrates' own aggression toward the state (expressed in critique), the idealization that limits what he will do in the name of criticizing or attacking the state, the idealization that tempers his dissidence.

But since this idealization itself is a sign of love, we may also read Socrates as explicitly, perhaps even deliberately, working the ambivalence in love in such a way that the aggression has a productive field and is not only contoured by the attachment but made responsible by it, and put into its service. Recall that Socrates does not simply make a case for the importance of tolerating philosophical critique of the polity but rather casts this work, at least as he conducts it, as the ultimate form of citizenship. The very fact that Socrates affirms his fealty to the state through a philosophical inquiry into whether it would be just to escape his sentencing is a rhetorical demonstration of how his critical philosophical activity works in the service of his love of Athens. A citizen less committed to thoughtfulness might have fled, or cut a deal . . . as the patriotic scoundrels often do.

But if dissent is, potentially, a form of love, and if all love entails idealization, what might be the idealization entailed in relentless practices of dissent or critique? This is a question so complex that most of its provocation must be held for another essay. What can be acknowledged here is that idealization of an eternally deferred elsewhere, of a utopian version of one's polity, surely animates the work of the radical critic just as idealization of the existing state of things, or more often of a polity's past, animates the conservative patriot. What is interesting about the figure of Socrates is that he harbors both and in rather extreme fashion. However, cultivating these two idealizations at the extreme is not the only way the tension between critique and fealty can be managed. The tension might be maintained such that one feels for the limits to critique in part by avowing the attachment that fuels it, by affirming the love, e.g., of this America or of another America, behind the anger or disappointment. This is not to say that the attachment itself should be shielded from interrogation, but interrogating attachment and disavowing it are quite different matters.

If critique could be expressly tendered as an act of love, if it could be offered in a Socratic spirit, might it be received differently? Perhaps it would appear less threatening to those who, consciously or unconsciously, experience it as assaulting their love object and as undermining the collectivity rallied around this love object. And if it were received differently, if it were not castigated as disloyal, un-American, or destructive—and thus placed outside legitimate political discourse — perhaps this would incite popular critique itself to more thoughtful, less moralistic or rebellious codes of conduct. It might then inhabit the dignified and authoritative voice of belonging, rather than the moral screech of exclusion. It might also be proffered in the voice of love and desire (for a better nation) rather than the voice of rage, shame, or denunciation. Conversely, if ambivalence in love could be forthrightly avowed in the formation of civic loyalty, the level of idealization (aimed at binding and shouting down this ambivalence) could be substantially lowered and so also might the shouting be reduced. And if loyalty did not seem to require this shouting down of criticism, this refusal of thoughtfulness itself, then in turn might the way be opened for apprehending rich civic debate—even and perhaps especially in times of crisis—as harboring the potential to strengthen rather than undermine a democracy?

Michael Ignatieff, also thinking through Freud about questions of civic belonging, concludes that "we are only likely to love others more if we love ourselves a little less."[22] This view, I think, aptly characterizes the contemporary "cosmopolitan" antidote to problems thought to be posed by parochial attachments and fundamentalist passions, in short by nationalisms big and small. The larger, more worldly view, and hence the one to be counted on for peace, liberal civility, and tolerant co-existence, is thought to require a reduction of local zeals and loyalties, and a corresponding increase in moral and political detachment. But this formulation remains trapped within the zero-sum Freudian economy in which civilization is enhanced or advanced only by depriving Eros of ever more gratification. I am suggesting a somewhat different route, one that brings reason and consciousness to practices of love rather than keeping them forever sequestered from one another, rather than asking reason to displace love on the one hand or barring love from reason and thoughtfulness on the other. This would involve developing political self-consciousness about the nature of civic love and developing as well practices to counter the potential destructiveness and anti-democratic energies and affects of such love. Specifically, it would require (1) avowing the aggression and ambivalence in love, and developing less dangerous outlets for the former and political lexicons that harbor the latter; (2) reckoning with the particular difficulties of group love and tracking the internal idealizations and external demonizations that arise to finesse these difficulties; and (3) coming to terms with the lack of identity and unity in civic love over space and time so as to be able to grasp how certain kinds of civic fervor arise to force oneness and permanence where they do not naturally inhere. Habits of political discourse that thematized these phenomena, or even simply monitored their effects, would not only reduce animosity toward dissent in times of crisis, but help to reset dimensions of the typically imagined trade-off between national security and democracy, between a democratic polity's strength and the polyvocality that signifies democracy itself. Above all, such discourse could articulate possibilities for a love of country oriented toward a thoughtful and empowered rather than passive citizenry, a love of democratic traditions and practices rather than nation-state power.

THREE

■ ■ ■ ■

NEOLIBERALISM AND THE END
OF LIBERAL DEMOCRACY

I T IS commonplace to speak of the present regime in the United States
as a neoconservative one, and to cast as a consolidated "neocon" project present efforts to intensify U.S. military capacity, increase U.S.
global hegemony, dismantle the welfare state, retrench civil liberties,
eliminate the right to abortion and affirmative action, re-Christianize the
state, deregulate corporations, gut environmental protections, reverse
progressive taxation, reduce education spending while increasing
prison budgets, and feather the nests of the rich while criminalizing the
poor. I do not contest the existence of a religious-political project known
as neoconservatism or challenge the appropriateness of understanding
many of the links between these objectives in terms of a neoconservative
agenda. However, I want to think to one side of this agenda in order to
consider our current predicament in terms of a neoliberal political rationality, a rationality that exceeds particular positions on particular issues
and that undergirds important features of the Clinton decade as well as
the Reagan-Bush years. Further, I want to consider the way that this rationality is emerging as governmentality—a mode of governance en-
compassing but not limited to the state, and one that produces subjects,
forms of citizenship and behavior, and a new organization of the social.[1]

ECONOMIC LIBERALISM, POLITICAL LIBERALISM,
AND WHAT IS THE NEO IN NEOLIBERALISM

In ordinary parlance, neoliberalism refers to the repudiation of Keynesian welfare state economics and the ascendance of the Chicago School
of political economy—von Hayek, Friedman, and others. In popular

usage, neoliberalism is equated with a radically free market: maximized competition and free trade achieved through economic deregulation, elimination of tariffs, and a range of monetary and social policies favorable to business and indifferent toward poverty, social deracination, cultural decimation, long-term resource depletion, and environmental destruction. Neoliberalism is most often invoked in relation to the Third World, referring either to NAFTA-like schemes that increase the vulnerability of poor nations to the vicissitudes of globalization or to International Monetary Fund and World Bank policies that, through financing packages attached to "restructuring" requirements, yank the chains of every aspect of Third World existence, including political institutions and social formations. For progressives, neoliberalism is thus a pejorative not only because it conjures economic policies that sustain or deepen local poverty and the subordination of peripheral to core nations, but also because it is compatible with, and sometimes even productive of, authoritarian, despotic, paramilitaristic, and corrupt state forms as well as agents within civil society.

While these referents capture important effects of neoliberalism, they also reduce neoliberalism to a bundle of economic policies with inadvertent political and social consequences: they fail to address the *political rationality* that both organizes these policies and reaches beyond the market. Moreover, these referents do not capture the *neo* in neoliberalism, tending instead to treat the contemporary phenomenon as little more than a revival of classical liberal political economy. Finally, they obscure the specifically political register of neoliberalism in the First World: that is, its powerful erosion of liberal democratic institutions and practices in places like the United States. My concern in this essay is with these neglected dimensions of neoliberalism.

One of the more incisive accounts of neoliberal political rationality comes from a surprising quarter: Michel Foucault is not generally heralded as a theorist of liberalism or of political economy. Yet Foucault's 1978 and 1979 Collège de France lectures, long unpublished,[2] consisted of his critical analysis of two groups of neoliberal economists: the *Ordo*-liberal school in postwar Germany (so named because its members, originally members of the Freiburg School, published mainly in the journal *Ordo*) and the Chicago School that arose midcentury in the United States. Thanks to the German sociologist Thomas Lemke, we have an excellent summary and interpretation of Foucault's lectures on neoliberalism; in what follows I will draw extensively from Lemke's work.[3]

It may be helpful, before beginning a consideration of neoliberalism as a political rationality, to mark the conventional difference between political and economic liberalism—a difference especially confusing for Americans for whom "liberal" tends to signify a progressive political viewpoint and, in particular, support for the welfare state and other New Deal institutions, along with relatively high levels of political and legal intervention in the social sphere.[4] In addition, given the contemporary phenomena of both neoconservatism and neoliberalism, and the association of both with the political right, ours is a time of often bewildering political nomenclature.[5] Briefly, then, in *economic* thought, liberalism contrasts with mercantilism on one side and Keynesianism or socialism on the other; its classical version refers to a maximization of free trade and competition achieved by minimum interference from political institutions. In the history of *political* thought, while individual liberty remains a touchstone, liberalism signifies an order in which the state exists to secure the freedom of individuals on a formally egalitarian basis. A liberal political order may harbor either liberal or Keynesian economic policies—it may lean in the direction of maximizing liberty (its politically "conservative" tilt) or of maximizing equality (its politically "liberal" tilt), but in contemporary political parlance, it is no more or less a liberal democracy because of one leaning or the other. Indeed, the American convention of referring to advocates of the welfare state as political liberals is especially peculiar, given that American conservatives generally hew more closely to both the classical economic and the political doctrines of liberalism—it turns the meaning of liberalism in the direction of *liberality* rather than *liberty*.

For our purposes, what is crucial is that *the liberalism in what has come to be called neoliberalism refers to liberalism's economic variant*, recuperating selected pre-Keynesian assumptions about the generation of wealth and its distribution, rather than to liberalism as a political doctrine, as a set of political institutions, or as political practices. The *neo* in neoliberalism, however, establishes these principles on a significantly different analytic basis from those set forth by Adam Smith, as will become clear below. Moreover, neoliberalism is not simply a set of economic policies; it is not only about facilitating free trade, maximizing corporate profits, and challenging welfarism. Rather, neoliberalism carries a social analysis that, when deployed as a form of governmentality, reaches from the soul of the citizen-subject to education policy to practices of empire. Neoliberal rationality, while foregrounding the market, is not only or even primarily focused on the economy; it involves *extending and disseminating market values to all institutions and social action*, even as the market itself remains a distinctive player. This essay explores the *political* implications of neoliberal rationality for liberal democracy—the implications of the political rationality corresponding to, legitimating, and legitimated by the neoliberal turn.

While Lemke, following Foucault, is careful to mark some of the differences between *Ordo*-liberal thought and its successor and radicalizer, the Chicago School, I will be treating contemporary neoliberal political rationality without attending to these differences in some of its source material. A rich genealogy of neoliberalism as it is currently practiced—one that mapped and contextualized the contributions of the two schools of political economy, traced the ways that rational choice theory differentially adhered and evolved in the various social sciences and their governmental applications, and described the interplay of all these currents with developments in capital over the past half century—would be quite useful. But this essay is not such a genealogy. Rather, my aim is to consider our current political predicament in terms of neoliberal political rationality, whose chief characteristics are enumerated below.

1. The political sphere, along with every other dimension of contemporary existence, is submitted to an economic rationality; or, put the other way around, not only is the human being configured exhaustively as *homo œconomicus*, but all dimensions of human life are cast in terms of a market rationality. While this entails submitting every action and policy to considerations of profitability, equally important is the production of all human and institutional action as rational entrepreneurial action, conducted according to a calculus of utility, benefit, or satisfaction against a microeconomic grid of scarcity, supply and demand, and moral value-neutrality. Neoliberalism does not simply assume that all aspects of social, cultural, and political life can be reduced to such a calculus; rather, it develops institutional practices and rewards for enacting this vision. That is, through discourse and policy promulgating its criteria, neoliberalism produces rational actors and imposes a market rationale for decision making in all spheres. Importantly, then, neoliberalism involves a normative rather than ontological claim about the pervasiveness of economic rationality and it advocates the institution building, policies, and discourse development appropriate to such a claim. Neoliberalism is a constructivist project: it does not presume the ontological givenness of a thoroughgoing economic rationality for all domains of society but rather

takes as its task the development, dissemination, and institutionalization of such a rationality. This point is further developed in (2) below.

2. In contrast with the notorious laissez-faire and human propensity to "truck and barter" stressed by classical economic liberalism, neoliberalism does not conceive of either the market itself or rational economic behavior as purely natural. Both are constructed—organized by law and political institutions, and requiring political intervention and orchestration. Far from flourishing when left alone, the economy must be directed, buttressed, and protected by law and policy as well as by the dissemination of social norms designed to facilitate competition, free trade, and rational economic action on the part of every member and institution of society. In Lemke's account, "In the *Ordo*-liberal scheme, the market does not amount to a natural economic reality, with intrinsic laws that the art of government must bear in mind and respect; instead, the market can be constituted and kept alive only by dint of political interventions. . . . [C]ompetition, too, is not a natural fact. . . . [T]his fundamental economic mechanism can function only if support is forthcoming to bolster a series of conditions, and adherence to the latter must consistently be guaranteed by legal measures" (193).

The neoliberal formulation of the state and especially of specific legal arrangements and decisions as the precondition and ongoing condition of the market does not mean that the market is controlled by the state but precisely the opposite. The market is the organizing and regulative principle of the state and society, along three different lines:

a. The state openly responds to needs of the market, whether through monetary and fiscal policy, immigration policy, the treatment of criminals, or the structure of public education. In so doing, the state is no longer encumbered by the danger of incurring the legitimation deficits predicted by 1970s social theorists and political economists such as Nicos Poulantzas, Jürgen Habermas, and James O'Connor.[6] Rather, neoliberal rationality extended to the state itself indexes the state's success according to its ability to sustain and foster the market and ties state legitimacy to such success. This is a new form of legitimation, one that "founds a state," according to Lemke, and contrasts with the Hegelian and French revolutionary notion of the constitutional state as the emergent universal representative of the people. As Lemke describes Foucault's account of *Ordo*-liberal thinking, "economic liberty produces the legitimacy for a form of sovereignty limited to guaranteeing economic activity . . . a state that was no longer defined in terms of an historical mission but legitimated itself with reference to economic growth" (196).

b. The state itself is enfolded and animated by market rationality: that is, not simply profitability but a generalized calculation of cost and benefit becomes the measure of all state practices. Political discourse on all matters is framed in entrepreneurial terms; *the state must not simply concern itself with the market but think and behave like a market actor* across all of its functions, including law. [7]

c. Putting (a) and (b) together, the health and growth of the economy is *the* basis of state legitimacy, both because the state is forthrightly responsible for the health of the economy and because of the economic rationality to which state practices have been submitted. Thus, "It's the economy, stupid" becomes more than a campaign slogan; rather, it expresses the principle of the state's legitimacy and the basis for state action—from constitutional adjudication and campaign finance reform to welfare and education policy to foreign policy, including warfare and the organization of "homeland security."

3. The extension of economic rationality to formerly noneconomic domains and institutions reaches individual conduct, or, more precisely, prescribes the citizen-subject of a neoliberal order. Whereas classical liberalism articulated a distinction, and at times even a tension, among the criteria for individual moral, associational, and economic actions (hence the striking differences in tone, subject matter, and even prescriptions between Adam Smith's *Wealth of Nations* and his *Theory of Moral Sentiments*), neoliberalism normatively constructs and interpellates individuals as entrepreneurial actors in every sphere of life. It figures individuals as rational, calculating creatures whose moral autonomy is measured by their capacity for "self-care"—the ability to provide for their own needs and service their own ambitions. In making the individual fully responsible for her- or himself, neoliberalism equates moral responsibility with rational action; it erases the discrepancy between economic and moral behavior by configuring morality entirely as a matter of rational deliberation about costs, benefits, and consequences. But in so doing, it carries responsibility for the self to new heights: the rationally calculating individual bears full responsibility for the consequences of his or her action no matter how severe the constraints on this action—for example, lack of skills, education, and child care in a period of high unemployment and limited welfare benefits. Correspondingly, a "mismanaged life," the neoliberal appellation for failure to navigate impediments to prosperity, becomes a

new mode of depoliticizing social and economic powers and at the same time reduces political citizenship to an unprecedented degree of passivity and political complacency. The model neoliberal citizen is one who strategizes for her- or himself among various social, political, and economic options, not one who strives with others to alter or organize these options. A fully realized neoliberal citizenry would be the opposite of public-minded; indeed, it would barely exist as a public. The body politic ceases to be a body but is rather a group of individual entrepreneurs and consumers . . . which is, of course, exactly how voters are addressed in most American campaign discourse.[8] Other evidence for progress in the development of such a citizenry is not far from hand: consider the market rationality permeating universities today, from admissions and recruiting to the relentless consumer mentality of students as they consider university brand names, courses, and services, from faculty raiding and pay scales to promotion criteria.[9] Or consider the way in which consequential moral lapses (of a sexual or criminal nature) by politicians, business executives, or church and university administrators are so often apologized for as "mistakes in judgment," implying that it was the calculation that was wrong, not the act, actor, or rationale.

The state is not without a project in the making of the neoliberal subject. It attempts to construct prudent subjects through policies that organize such prudence: this is the basis of a range of welfare reforms such as workfare and single-parent penalties, changes in the criminal code such as the "three strikes law," and educational voucher schemes. Because neoliberalism casts rational action as a norm rather than an ontology, social policy is the means by which the state produces subjects whose compass is set entirely by their rational assessment of the costs and benefits of certain acts, whether those acts pertain to teen pregnancy, tax fraud, or retirement planning. The neoliberal citizen is calculating rather than rule abiding, a Benthamite rather than a Hobbesian. The state is one of many sites framing the calculations leading to social behaviors that keep costs low and productivity high.

This mode of governmentality (techniques of governing that exceed express state action and orchestrate the subject's conduct toward him- or herself) convenes a "free" subject who rationally deliberates about alternative courses of action, makes choices, and bears responsibility for the consequences of these choices. In this way, Lemke argues, "the state leads and controls subjects without being responsible for them"; as individual "entrepreneurs" in every aspect of life, subjects become wholly responsible for their well-being and citizenship is reduced to success in this entrepreneurship (201). Neoliberal subjects are controlled *through* their freedom—not simply, as thinkers from the Frankfurt School through Foucault have argued, because freedom within an order of domination can be an instrument of that domination, but because of neoliberalism's *moralization* of the consequences of this freedom. Such control also means that the withdrawal of the state from certain domains, followed by the privatization of certain state functions, does not amount to a dismantling of government but rather constitutes a technique of governing; indeed, it is the signature technique of neoliberal governance, in which rational economic action suffused throughout society replaces express state rule or provision. Neoliberalism shifts "the regulatory competence of the state onto 'responsible,' 'rational' individuals [with the aim of] encourag[ing] individuals to give their lives a specific entrepreneurial form" (Lemke, 202).

4. Finally, the suffusion of both the state and the subject with economic rationality has the effect of radically transforming and narrowing the criteria for good social policy vis-à-vis classical liberal democracy. Not only must social policy meet profitability tests, incite and unblock competition, and produce rational subjects, it obeys the entrepreneurial principle of "equal inequality for all" as it "multiples and expands entrepreneurial forms with the body social" (Lemke, 195). This is the principle that links the neoliberal governmentalization of the state with that of the social and the subject.

Taken together, the extension of economic rationality to all aspects of thought and activity, the placement of the state in forthright and direct service to the economy, the rendering of the state *tout court* as an enterprise organized by market rationality, the production of the moral subject as an entrepreneurial subject, and the construction of social policy according to these criteria might appear as a more intensive rather than fundamentally new form of the saturation of social and political realms by capital. That is, the political rationality of neoliberalism might be read as issuing from a stage of capitalism that simply underscores Marx's argument that capital penetrates and transforms every aspect of life—remaking everything in its image and reducing every value and activity to its cold rationale. All that would be new here is the flagrant and relentless submission of the state and the individual, the church and the university, morality, sex, marriage, and leisure practices to this rationale. Or better, the only novelty would be the recently achieved hegemony of rational choice theory in the human sciences, self-represented as an independent and objective branch of knowledge rather than an expression of the dominance of capital.

Another reading that would figure neoliberalism as continuous with the past would theorize it through Weber's rationalization thesis rather than Marx's argument about capital. The extension of market rationality to every sphere, and especially the reduction of moral and political judgment to a cost-benefit calculus, would represent precisely the evisceration of substantive values by instrumental rationality that Weber predicted as the future of a disenchanted world. Thinking and judging are reduced to instrumental calculation in Weber's "polar night of icy darkness"—there is no morality, no faith, no heroism, indeed no meaning outside the market.

Yet invaluable as Marx's theory of capital and Weber's theory of rationalization are in understanding certain aspects of neoliberalism, neither brings into view the historical-institutional rupture it signifies, the form of governmentality it replaces and the form it inaugurates, and hence the modalities of resistance it renders outmoded and those that must be developed if it is to be effectively challenged. Neoliberalism is not an inevitable historical development of capital and instrumental rationality; it is not the unfolding of laws of capital or of instrumental rationality suggested by a Marxist or Weberian analysis but represents instead a new and contingent organization and operation of both. Moreover, neither analysis articulates the shift neoliberalism heralds from relatively *differentiated* moral, economic, and political rationalities and venues in liberal democratic orders to their discursive and practical integration. Neoliberal governmentality undermines the relative autonomy of certain institutions—law, elections, the police, the public sphere—from one another and from the market, an independence that formerly sustained an interval and a tension between a capitalist political economy and a liberal democratic political system. The implications of this transformation are significant. Herbert Marcuse worried about the loss of a dialectical opposition *within* capitalism when it "delivers the goods"—that is, when, by the mid–twentieth century, a relatively complacent middle class had taken the place of the hard-laboring impoverished masses Marx depicted as the negating contradiction to the concentrated wealth of capital—but neoliberalism entails the erosion of oppositional political, moral, or subjective claims located *outside* capitalist rationality yet inside liberal democratic society, that is, the erosion of institutions, venues, and values organized by nonmarket rationalities in democracies. When democratic principles of governance, civil codes, and even religious morality are submitted to economic calculation, when no value or good stands outside of this calculus, then sources of opposition to, and mere modulation of, capitalist rationality disappear. This reminds us that however much a left analysis has identified a liberal political order with legitimating, cloaking, and mystifying the stratifications of society achieved by capitalism (and achieved as well by racial, sexual, and gender superordinations), it is also the case that liberal democratic principles of governance—liberalism as a political doctrine—have functioned as something of an antagonist to these stratifications. As Marx himself argued in "On the Jewish Question," formal political principles of equality and freedom (with their attendant promises of individual autonomy and dignity) figure an alternative vision of humanity and alternative social and moral referents to those of the capitalist order within which they are asserted. This is the Janus-face or at least Janus-potential of liberal democracy vis-à-vis a capitalist economy: while liberal democracy encodes, reflects, and legitimates capitalist social relations, it simultaneously resists, counters, and tempers them.

Put simply, what liberal democracy has provided over the past two centuries is a modest ethical gap between economy and polity. Even as liberal democracy converges with many capitalist values (property rights, individualism, Hobbesian assumptions underneath all contracts, etc.), the formal distinction it establishes between moral and political principles on the one hand and the economic order on the other has also served to insulate citizens against the ghastliness of life exhaustively ordered by the market and measured by market values. It is this gap that a neoliberal political rationality closes as it submits every aspect of political and social life to economic calculation: asking not, for example, what liberal constitutionalism stands for, what moral or political values it protects and preserves, but rather what efficacy or profitability constitutionalism promotes . . . or interdicts.

Liberal democracy cannot be submitted to neoliberal political governmentality and survive. There is nothing in liberal democracy's basic institutions or values—from free elections, representative democracy, and individual liberties equally distributed to modest power-sharing or even more substantive political participation—that inherently meets the test of serving economic competitiveness or inherently withstands a cost-benefit analysis. And it is liberal democracy that is going under in the present moment, even as the flag of American "democracy" is being planted everywhere it can find or create soft ground. (That "democracy" is the rubric under which so much antidemocratic imperial and domestic policy is enacted suggests that we are in an interregnum—or, more precisely, that neoliberalism borrows extensively from the old regime to legitimate itself even as it also develops and disseminates new codes of legitimacy. More about this below.)

Nor is liberal democracy a temporary casualty of recent events or of a neoconservative agenda. As the foregoing account of neoliberal governmentality suggests, while post-9/11 international and domestic policy may have both hastened and highlighted the erosion of liberal democratic institutions and principles, this erosion is not simply the result of a national security strategy or even of the Bush administration's unprecedented indifference to the plight of the poor, civil liberties, law valued as principle rather than tactic, or conventional liberal democratic criteria for legitimate foreign policy.[10] My argument here is twofold. First, neoliberal rationality has not caused but rather has facilitated the dismantling of democracy during the current national security crisis. Democratic values and institutions are trumped by a cost-benefit and efficiency rationale for practices ranging from government secrecy (even government lying) to the curtailment of civil liberties. Second, the post-9/11 period has brought the ramifications of neoliberal rationality into sharp focus, largely through practices and policies that progressives assail as hypocrisies, lies, or contradictions but that may be better understood as neoliberal policies and actions taking shape under the legitimating cloth of a liberal democratic discourse increasingly void of substance.

The Bush administration's imperial adventures in Afghanistan and Iraq clearly borrowed extensively from the legitimating rhetoric of democracy. Not only were both wars undertaken as battles for "our way of life" against regimes said to harbor enemies (terrorists) or dangers (weapons of mass destruction) to that way of life, but both violations of national sovereignty were justified by the argument that democracy could and ought to take shape in those places—each nation is said to need liberation from brutal and despotic rule. The standard left criticism of the first justification is that "our way of life" is more seriously threatened by a politics of imperialism and by certain policies of homeland security than by these small nations. But this criticism ignores the extent to which "our way of life" is being figured not in a classically liberal democratic but in a neoliberal idiom: that is, as the ability of the entrepreneurial subject and state to rationally plot means and ends and the ability of the state to secure the conditions, at home and abroad, for a market rationality and subjectivity by removing their impediments (whether Islamic fundamentalism or excessive and arbitrary state sovereignty in the figure of Saddam Hussein). Civil liberties are perfectly expendable within this conception of "our way of life"; unlike property rights, they are largely irrelevant to *homo œconomicus*. Their attenuation or elimination does not falsify the project of protecting democracy in its neoliberal mode.

The Left criticized the second justification, that the United States could or ought to liberate Afghanistan from the Taliban and Iraq from Hussein, as both hypocritical (the United States had previously funded and otherwise propped up both regimes) and disingenuous (U.S. foreign policy has never rested on the principle of developing democracy and was not serious about the project in these settings). Again, however, translated into neoliberal terms, "democracy," here or there, does not signify a set of independent political institutions and civic practices comprising equality, freedom, autonomy and the principle of popular sovereignty but rather indicates only a state and subjects organized by market rationality. Indeed, democracy could even be understood as a code word for availability to this rationality; removal of the Taliban and Baath party pave the way to that availability, and democracy is simply the name of the regime, conforming to neoliberal requirements, that must replace them. When Paul Bremer, the U.S.-appointed interim governor of Iraq, declared on May 26, 2003 (just weeks after the sacking of Baghdad and four days after the UN lifted economic sanctions), that Iraq was "open for business," he made clear exactly how democracy would take shape in post-Saddam Iraq. Duty-free imported goods poured into the country, finishing off many local Iraqi businesses already damaged by the war. Multinationals tumbled over themselves to get a piece of the action, and foreign direct investment to replace and privatize state industry was described by the corporate executives advising the Bush administration as the "answer to all of Iraq's problems."[11] The question of democratic institutions, as Bremer made clear by scrapping early plans to form an interim Iraqi government in favor of installing his own team of advisers, was at best secondary to the project of privatizing large portions of the economy and outsourcing the business of policing a society in rubble, chaos, and terror occasioned by the combination of ongoing military skirmishes and armed local gangs.[12]

It is not news that replacements for the Taliban and the Baath regimes need not be rights-based, formally egalitarian, representative, or otherwise substantively democratic in order to serve the purposes of global capitalism or the particular geopolitical interests of the United States. Nor is it news that the replacements of these regimes need not be administered by the Afghans or Iraqis themselves to satisfy American and global capitalist purposes and interests, though the residues of old-fashioned democracy inside the legitimation project of neoliberalism make even puppet or faux rule by an appointed governing council, or by officials elected in severely compromised election conditions, ideologically preferable to full-fledged directorship by the American occupation. What is striking, however, is the boldness of a raw market approach to political problem solving, the extent to which radical privatization schemes and a flourishing market economy built on foreign investment are offered not simply as the path to democracy but as the name and the measure of democracy in these nations, a naming and measuring first appearing in post-1989 Eastern Europe a decade earlier. Not only are democratic institutions largely irrelevant—and at times even impediments—to neoliberal governmentality, but the success of such governmentality does not depend on the question of whether it is locally administered or externally imposed. Market rationality knows no culture or country, and administrators are, as the economists say, fungible. Indeed, at this juncture in the displacement of liberal democracy by neoliberal governmentality, the question is how much legitimacy neoliberal governance requires from a democratic vocabulary—how much does neoliberalism have to cloak itself in liberal democratic discourse and work with liberal democratic institutions? This is less a theoretical than a historical-empirical question about how deeply and extensively neoliberal rationality has taken hold as ideology, that is, how much and where neoliberal governance can legitimate itself in its own terms, without borrowing from other discourses. (Neoliberalism can become dominant as governmentality without being dominant as ideology—the former refers to governing practices and the latter to a popular order of belief that may or may not be fully in line with the former, and that may even be a site of resistance to it.) Clearly, a rhetoric of democracy and the shell of liberal democratic institutions remain more important in the imperial heartland than in recently "liberated" or conquered societies with few if any democratic traditions of legitimacy. However, the fact that George W. Bush retains the support of the majority of the American people, despite his open flaunting of democratic principles amid a failing economy and despite, too, evidence that the public justification for invading Iraq relied on cooked intelligence, suggests that neoliberalism has taken deep hold in the homeland. Particularly striking is the number of pundits who have characterized this willful deceit of the people as necessary rather than criminal, as a means to a rational end, thereby reminding us that one of the more dangerous features of neoliberal evisceration of a non-market morality lies in undercutting the basis for judging government actions by any criteria other than expedience.[13]

Just as neoliberal governmentality reduces the tension historically borne by the state between democratic values and the needs of capital as it openly weds the state to capital and resignifies democracy as ubiquitous entrepreneurialism, so neoliberalism also smooths an old wrinkle in the fabric of liberal democratic foreign policy between domestic political values and international interests. During the cold war, political progressives could use American sanctimony about democracy to condemn international actions that propped up or installed authoritarian regimes and overthrew popularly elected leaders in the Third World. The divergence between strategic international interests and democratic ideology produced a potential legitimation problem for foreign policy, especially as applied to Southeast Asia and Central and Latin America. Neoliberalism, by redefining democracy as thoroughgoing market rationality in state and society, a redefinition abetted by the postcommunist "democratization" process in Eastern Europe, largely eliminates that problem. Certainly human rights talk is ubiquitous in global democracy discourse, but not since Jimmy Carter's ill-fated efforts to make human rights a substantive dimension of foreign policy have they served as more than window dressing for neoliberal adventures in democracy.

MOURNING LIBERAL DEMOCRACY

An assault on liberal democratic values and institutions has been plainly evident in recent events: civil liberties undermined by the USA Patriot Acts and the Total Information Awareness (later renamed Total Terror Awareness) scheme, Oakland police shooting wood and rubber bullets at peaceful antiwar protesters, a proposed Oregon law to punish all civil disobedience as terrorism (replete with twenty five-year jail terms), and McCarthyite deployments of patriotism to suppress ordinary dissent and its iconography. It is evident as well in the staging of aggressive imperial wars and ensuing occupations along with the continued dismantling of the welfare state and the progressive taxation schemes already diluted by the Reagan, G.H.W. Bush, and

Clinton administrations. It has been more subtly apparent in "softer" events, such as the de-funding of public education that led eighty four Oregon school districts to sheer almost a month off the school year in spring 2003 and delivered provisional pink slips to thousands of California teachers at the end of the 2002–03 academic year.[14] Or consider the debate about whether antiwar protests constituted unacceptable costs for a financially strapped cities—even many critics of current U.S. foreign policy expressed anger at peaceful civil disobedients over the expense and disruption they caused, implying that the value of public opinion and protest should be measured against its dollar cost.[15] Together these phenomena suggest a transformation of American liberal democracy into a political and social form for which we do not yet have a name, a form organized by a combination of neoliberal governmentality and imperial world politics, shaped in the short run by global economic and security crises. They indicate a form in which an imperial agenda is able to take hold precisely because the domestic soil has been loosened for it by neoliberal rationality.

This form is not fascism or totalitarian as we have known them historically, nor are these labels likely to prove helpful in identifying or criticizing it.[16] Rather, this is a political condition in which the substance of many of the significant features of constitutional and representative democracy have been gutted, jettisoned, or end-run, even as they continue to be promulgated ideologically, serving as a foil and shield for their undoing and for the doing of death elsewhere. These features include civil liberties equally distributed and protected; a press and other journalistic media minimally free from corporate ownership on one side and state control on the other; uncorrupted and unbought elections; quality public education oriented, *inter alia*, to producing the literacies relevant to informed and active citizenship; government openness, honesty, and accountability; a judiciary modestly insulated from political and commercial influence; separation of church and state; and a foreign policy guided at least in part by the rationale of protecting these domestic values. None of these constitutive elements of liberal democracy was ever fully realized in its short history—they have always been compromised by a variety of economic and social powers, from white supremacy to capitalism. And liberal democracies in the First World have always required other peoples to pay—politically, socially, and economically—for what these societies have enjoyed; that is, there has always been a colonially and imperially inflected gap between what has been valued in the core and what has been required from the periphery. So it is important to be precise here. Ours is not the first time in which elections have been bought, manipulated, and even engineered by the courts, the first time the press has been slavish to state and corporate power, the first time the United States has launched an aggressive assault on a sovereign nation or threatened the entire world with its own weapons of mass destruction. What is unprecedented about this time is the extent to which basic principles and institutions of democracy are becoming nothing other than ideological shells concealing their opposite as well as the extent to which these principles and institutions even as values are being abandoned by large parts of the American population. Elements in this transformation include the development of the most secretive government in fifty years (the gutting of the Freedom of Information Act was one of the quiet early accomplishments of the G. W. Bush administration, the "classified" status of its more than 1,000 contracts with Halliburton one of its more recent); the plumping of corporate wealth combined with the reduction of social spending for limiting the economic vulnerability of the poor and middle classes; a bought, consolidated, and muffled press that willingly cooperates in its servitude (emblematic in this regard is the Judith Miller (non)scandal, in which the star *New York Times* journalist wittingly reported Pentagon propaganda about Iraqi WMDs as journalistically discovered fact); and intensified policing in every corner of American life—airports, university admissions offices, mosques, libraries, workplaces—a policing undertaken both by official agents of the state and by an interpellated citizenry. A potentially permanent "state of emergency" combined with an infinitely expandable rhetoric of patriotism overtly legitimates undercutting the Bill of Rights and legitimates as well abrogation of conventional democratic principles in setting foreign policy, principles that include respect for nation-state sovereignty and reasoned justifications for war. But behind these rhetorics there is another layer of discourse facilitating the dismantling of liberal democratic institutions and practices: a governmentality of neoliberalism that eviscerates nonmarket morality and thus erodes the root of democracy in principle at the same time that it raises the status of profit and expediency as the criteria for policy making.

There is much that is disturbing in the emergence of neoliberal governmentality and a great deal more work to do in theorizing its contribution to the organization and possibilities in current and future political life in the United States. In particular, as I suggested at the outset of this essay, filling in the contemporary political picture would require mapping the convergences and tensions between a (nonpartisan) neoliberal governmentality on the one hand and the specific agendas of Clintonian centrists and Reagan-Bush neoconservatives on the other. It would require exploring the continued efficacy of political rhetorics of morality and principle as neoliberalism voids the substance of and undercuts the need for extramarket morality. It would require discerning what distinguishes neoliberal governmentality from old-fashioned corporatism and old-fashioned political realism. It would require examining the contradictory political imperatives delivered by the market and set as well by the tensions between nation-state interests and globalized capitalism indifferent to states and sovereignty. And it would require examining the points at which U.S. imperial policies converge with and diverge from or even conflict with neoliberal governmentality.

By way of conclusion, however, I leave aside these questions to reflect briefly on the implications for the Left of neoliberalism's erosion of liberal democracy. While leftists of the past quarter century were rarely as antagonistic to liberal democracy as the Old Left, neither did we fully embrace it; at times we resented and railed against it, and certainly we harbored an aim to transform it into something else—social democracy or some form of radical democracy. So the Left is losing something it never loved, or at best was highly ambivalent about. We are also losing a site of criticism and political agitation—we criticized liberal democracy not only for its hypocrisy and ideological trickery but also for its institutional and rhetorical embedding of bourgeois, white, masculinist, and heterosexual superordination at the heart of humanism. Whatever loose identity we had as a Left took shape in terms of a differentiation from liberalism's willful obliviousness to social stratification and injury that were glossed and hence secured by its formal juridical categories of liberty and equality.

Still, liberalism, as Gayatri Spivak once wrote in a very different context, is also that which one "cannot not want" (given the other historical possibilities, given the current historical meaning of its deprivation). Even here, though, the desire is framed as roundabout and against itself, as Spivak's artful double negative indicates. It indicates a dependency we are not altogether happy about, an organization of desire we wish were otherwise. What might be the psychic/social/intellectual implications for leftists of losing this vexed object of attachment? What are the possible trajectories for a melancholic incorporation of that vard which one is openly ambivalent; or perhaps even hostile, sentful, rebellious?

Freud posits melancholy as occasioned by ambivalence, though the ambivalence may be more unconsciously sustained than I am suggesting is the case for the Left's relationship to liberal democracy. More precisely, Freud's focus in theorizing melancholy is love that does not know or want to avow its hostility, whereas the task before us is to consider hostility that does not know or want to avow its love or dependency. Still, Freud's thinking about melancholia remains useful here as a theory of loss amid ambivalent attachment and dependence and a theory of identity formation at the site of an ungrievable passion or attachment. It reminds us to consider how left melancholia about liberal democracy would not just be a problematic affect but would constitute a formation of the Left itself.

Incorporating the death of a loathed object to which one was nonetheless attached often takes the form of acting out the loathed qualities of the object. I once had an acquaintance whose much-despised and abusive father died. While my friend overtly rejoiced at his passing, in the ensuing months she engaged in extraordinary outbursts of verbal and physical abuse toward friends and colleagues, even throwing things at them as she had described her father throwing household objects during her childhood. Another friend buried, after years of illness, a childish, hysterical, histrionic, and demanding mother, one who relentlessly produced herself as a victim amid her own aggressive demands. Relieved as my friend was to have done with this parent, what should emerge over the following year but exactly such tendencies in her own relationships? So this is one danger: that we would act out to keep alive those aspects of the political formation we are losing, that we would take up and perform liberal democracy's complacencies, cruelties, or duplicities, stage them in our own work and thinking. This behavior would issue in part from the need to preserve the left identity and project that took shape at the site of liberal democracy, and in part from ambivalence about liberal democracy itself. In response to the loss of an object both loved and loathed, in which only the loathing or contempt is avowed, melancholy sustains the loved object, and continues to provide a cover for the love—a continued means of disavowing it—by incorporating and performing the loathsomeness.

There are other ways ambivalently structured loss can take shape as melancholic, including the straightforward possibility of idealizing a lost object as it was never idealized when alive. Straightforward, perhaps, but not simple, for this affect also involves remorse for a past of not loving the object well enough and self-reproach for ever having wished for its death or replacement. As idealization fueled by guilt, this affect also entails heightened aggression toward challenges or challengers to the idealization. In this guilt, anxiety, and defensiveness over the loss of liberal democracy, we would feel compelled to defend basic principles of liberalism or simply defend liberalism as a whole *in a liberal way*, that is, we would give up being critical of liberalism and, in doing so, give up being left. Freud identifies this surrender of identity upon the death of an ambivalent object as the suicidal wish in melancholia,[17] a wish abetted in our case by a more general disorientation about what the Left is or stands for today. Evidence for such a surrender in the present extends from our strikingly unnuanced defenses of free speech, privacy, and other civil liberties to the staging of antiwar protests as "patriotic" through the iconography of the American flag. Often explained as what the Left must do when public discourse moves rightward, such accounts presume a single political continuum, ranged from extreme left to extreme right, in which liberals and conservatives are nothing more than the moderate versions of the extremes (communists and fascists). Not only does the model of the continuum reduce the variety of political possibility in modernity to matters of degree rather than kind, it erases the distinctiveness of a left critique and vision. Just as today's neoliberals bear little in common with traditional conservatives, so the Left has traditionally stood for a set of values and possibilities qualitatively different from those of welfare state liberals. Times of alliance and spheres of overlap obviously exist, but a continuum does not capture the nature of these convergences and tactical linkages any better than it captures the differences between, for example, a liberal commitment to rights-based equality and a left commitment to emancipating the realm of production, or between a liberal enthusiasm for the welfare state and a left critique of its ideological and regulatory dimensions. So the idea that leftists must automatically defend liberal political values when they are on the ropes, while sensible from a liberal perspective, does not facilitate a left challenge to neoliberalism if the Left still wishes to advocate in the long run for something other than liberal democracy in a capitalist socioeconomic order.

Of course, there are aspects of liberal democracy that the Left has come to value and incorporate into its own vision of the good society—for example, an array of individual liberties that are largely unrelated to the freedom from domination promised by transforming the realm of production. But articulating this renewed left vision differs from defending civil liberties in liberal terms, a defense that itself erases a left project as it consigns it to something outside those terms. Similarly, patriotism and flag-waving are surely at odds with a left formulation of justice, even as love of America, represented through icons other than the flag or through narratives other than "supporting the troops," might well have a part in this formulation. Finally, not only does defending liberal democracy in liberal terms sacrifice a left vision, but this sacrifice discredits the Left by tacitly reducing it to nothing more than a permanent objection to the existing regime. It renders the Left a party of complaint rather than a party with an alternative political, social, and economic vision.

Still, if we are slipping from liberalism to fascism, and if radical democracy or socialism is nowhere on the political horizon, don't we have to defend liberal democratic institutions and values? Isn't this the lesson of Weimar? I have labored to suggest that this is not the right diagnosis of our predicament: it does not grasp what is at stake in neoliberal governmentality—which is not fascism—nor on what grounds it might be challenged. Indeed, the left defense of the welfare state in the 1980s, which seemed to stem from precisely such an analysis—"if we can't have socialism, at least we should preserve welfare state capitalism"—backfired from just such a misdiagnosis. On the one hand, rather than articulating an emancipatory vision that included the eradication rather than regulation of poverty, the Left appeared aligned with big government, big spending, and misplaced compassion for those construed as failing to give their lives proper entrepreneurial shape. On the other hand, the welfare state was dismantled on grounds that had almost nothing to do with the terms of liberal democracy and everything to do with neoliberal economic and political rationality. We are not simply in the throes of a right-wing or conservative positioning within liberal democracy but rather at the threshold of a different political formation, one that conducts and legitimates itself on different grounds from liberal democracy even as it does not immediately divest itself of the name. It is a formation that is developing a domestic imperium correlative with a global one, achieved through a secretive and remarkably agentic state; through corporatized media, schools, and prisons; and through a variety of technologies for intensified local administrative, regulatory, and police powers. It is a formation made possible by the production of citizens as individual entrepreneurial actors across all dimensions of their lives, by the reduction of civil society to a domain for exercising this entrepreneurship, and by the figuration of the state as a firm whose products are rational individual subjects, an expanding economy, national security, and global power.

This formation produces a twofold challenge for the Left. First, it compels us to consider the implications of losing liberal democracy and especially its implications for our own work by learning what the Left has depended on and demanded from liberal democracy, which aspects of it have formed the basis of our critiques of it, rebellions against it, and identity based on differentiation from it. We may also need to mourn liberal democracy, avowing our ambivalent attachment to it, our need for it, our mix of love and hostility toward it. The aim of this work is framed by the second challenge, that of devising intelligent left strategies for challenging the neoliberal political-economic formation now taking shape and an intelligent left countervision to this formation.

A half century ago, Marcuse argued that capitalism had eliminated a revolutionary subject (the proletariat) representing the negation of capitalism; consequently, he insisted, the Left had to derive and cultivate anticapitalist principles, possibilities, and agency from capitalism's constitutive *outside*. That is, the Left needed to tap the desires— not for wealth or goods but for beauty, love, mental and physical well-being, meaningful work, and peace—manifestly unmet within a capitalist order and to appeal to those desires as the basis for rejecting and replacing the order. No longer could *economic* contradictions of capitalism inherently fuel opposition to it; rather, opposition had to be founded in an alternative table of values. Today, the problem Marcuse diagnosed has expanded from capitalism to liberal democracy: oppositional consciousness cannot be generated from liberal democracy's false promises and hypocrisies. The space between liberal democratic ideals and lived realities has ceased to be exploitable, because liberal democracy itself is no longer the most salient discourse of political legitimacy and the good life. Put the other way around, the politically exploitable hollowness in formal promises of freedom and equality has largely vanished to the extent that both freedom and equality have been redefined by neoliberalism. Similarly, revealed connections between political and economic actors—not merely bought politicians but arrangements of mutual profiteering between corporate America and its political elite—do not incite outrage at malfeasance, corruption, or injustice but appear instead as a potentially rational set of linkages between state and economy. Thus, from the "scandal" of Enron to the "scandal" of Vice President Cheney delivering Iraq to Halliburton to clean up and rebuild, there is no scandal. There is only market rationality, a rationality that can encompass even a modest amount of criminality but also treats close state-corporate ties as a potentially positive value—maximizing the aims of each—rather than as a conflict of interest.[18] Similarly, even as the Bush administration fails to come up with WMDs in Iraq and fails to be able to install order let alone democracy there, such deficiencies are irrelevant to the neoliberal criteria for success in that military episode. Indeed, even the scandal of Bush's installation as president by a politicized Supreme Court in 2000 was more or less ingested by the American people as business as usual, an ingestion that represents a shift from the expectation that the Supreme Court is independent of political influence to one that tacitly accepts its inclusion in the governmentality of neoliberalism. Similarly, John Poindexter, a key figure in the Iran-Contra affair and director of the proposed "Terrorism Information Awareness" program that would have put all Americans under surveillance, continued to have power and legitimacy at the Pentagon until the flap over the scheme to run a futures market on political violence in the Middle East. All three of these projects are instances of neoliberalism's indifference to democracy; only the last forced Poindexter into retirement.

These examples suggest that not only liberal democratic principles but democratic *morality* has been largely eviscerated—in neoliberal terms, each of these "scandals" is framed as a matter of miscalculation or political maneuvering rather than by right and wrong, truth or falsehood, institutional propriety or impropriety. Consequently, the Left cannot count on revealed deception, hypocrisies, interlocking directorates, featherbedding, or corruption to stir opposition to the existing regime. It cannot count on the expectation that moral principle undergirds political action or even on consistency as a value by which to judge state practices or aims. Much of the American public appeared indifferent to the fact that both the Afghan and Iraqi regimes targeted by Bush had previously been supported or even built by earlier U.S. foreign policy. It also appeared indifferent to the touting of the "liberation" of Afghan women as one of the great immediate achievements of the overthrow of the Taliban while the overthrow of the Baath regime set into motion an immediately more oppressive regime of gender in Iraq. The inconsistency does not matter much, because political reasons and reasoning that exceed or precede neoliberal criteria have ceased to matter much. This is serious political nihilism, which no mere defense of free speech and privacy, let alone securing the right to gay marriage or an increase in the minimum wage, will reverse.

What remains for the Left, then, is to challenge emerging neoliberal governmentality in Euro-Atlantic states with an alternative vision of the good, one that rejects *homo œconomicus* as the norm of the human *and* rejects this norm's correlative formations of economy, society, state, and (non)morality. In its barest form, this would be a vision in which justice would center not on maximizing individual wealth or rights but on developing and enhancing the capacity of citizens to share power and hence to collaboratively govern themselves. In such an order, rights and elections would be the background rather than token of democracy; or better, rights would function to safeguard the individual against radical democratic enthusiasms but would not themselves signal the presence or constitute the principle of democracy. Instead, a left vision of justice would focus on practices and institutions of popular power; a modestly egalitarian distribution of wealth and access to institutions; an incessant reckoning with all forms of power—social, economic, political, and even psychic; a long view of the fragility and finitude of nonhuman nature; and the importance of both meaningful activity and hospitable dwellings to human flourishing. However differently others might place the accent marks, none of these values can be derived from neoliberal rationality or meet neoliberal criteria for the good. The drive to develop and promulgate such a counterrationality—a different figuration of human beings, citizenship, economic life, and the political—is critical both to the long labor of fashioning a more just future and to the immediate task of challenging the deadly policies of the imperial American state.

FOUR

▪ ▪ ▪ ▪

AT THE EDGE: THE FUTURE
OF POLITICAL THEORY

Here lies the vocation of those who preserve our understanding of
past theories, who sharpen our sense of the subtle, complex interplay between political experience and thought, and who preserve
our memory of the agonizing efforts of intellect to restate the
possibilities and threats posed by political dilemmas of the past.
—SHELDON S. WOLIN, "Political Theory as a Vocation"

In the same way in which the great transformation of the first
industrial revolution destroyed the social and political structures
as well as the legal categories of the ancien regime, terms such
as *sovereignty, right, nation, people, democracy, and general will* by
now refer to a reality that no longer has anything to do with
what these concepts used to designate—and those who continue
to use these concepts uncritically literally do not know what they
are talking about.
—GIORGIO AGAMBEN, *Means without Ends: Notes on Politics*

Looking obliquely at the edges of things, where they come
together with other things, can tell you as much about them,
often, as can looking at them directly, intently, straight on.
—CLIFFORD GEERTZ, "The Near East in the Far East"

CONTEMPORARY critical theory teaches that identity is created
through borders and oppositions. The outside constructs the
inside and then hides this work of fabrication in an entity that
appears to give birth to itself. Thus to inquire "What is political theory?"
is to ask about its constitutive outside as well as its techniques of

dissimulating this constitution. What does political theory position itself against and by what discursive means? What does it imagine itself not to be, to be different from? What epistemological, stylistic, and ontological conceits denote its significant others, its scenes of alterity?

Explicit answers to these questions have varied over the several millennia of political theory in the West. For Socrates, the epic poets and the Sophists contoured the edges of political theory; for Machiavelli, it was Christian moralists; for Hobbes, the scholastics; for Nietzsche, moral theorists; for Weber, political ideologues; for Hannah Arendt, social and economic theory; for Sheldon Wolin, methodism; for Isaiah Berlin, science. This partial list reminds us that what is cast out is also that which rivals or displaces the enterprise, or contains the specter of its colonization. What defines political theory for any epoch or thinker is also conceived, at least in part, as threatening its dissolution. This becomes even clearer when we leave the consideration of epistemological concerns for ontological ones: across its disparate modalities, political theory takes its bearings from a tacit presumption of the relative boundedness and autonomy of the political. The existence of political theory qua political theory has depended heavily on defining the political as distinguishable (if not distinct) from the economic, the social, the cultural, the natural, and the private/domestic/familial. Nor does content exhaust this project of differentiation: political life is also tacitly circumscribed by its theorists in terms of a distinct ethos or sensibility, differentiated (albeit not necessarily sequestered) from the emotional, the psychic, the erotic, the poetic, the literary, and, at times, the moral. For political theory to claim singularity and claim propriety over a territory of concern, it must set itself off from these other domains, practices, and sensibilities. But like political theory's epistemological others, each laps at the shore of the political, promising to subvert or undo it if certain policing measures are not undertaken.

All of which is to say the familiar: if the very existence of political theory depends on contingent designations of what is not political and what is not theoretical, then political theory is a fiction, constituted by invented distinctions and a range of rivalries and conceits, each of which is mutable and puncturable, and which vary across time and place, not to mention investment and interest. To identify political theory's contrived nature, however, does not reduce or devalue the enterprise; rather, such identification helps set the stage for considering the possibilities and challenges it faces in a particular time and place. An understanding of what political theory arrays itself against today, how it differentiates itself from what is intellectually proximate to it, and what wolves it fears at its door may help us grasp not only what political theory imagines itself to be and to be for but also what anxieties and uncertainties it has about this identity, and what limits it places on itself to maintain coherence and purpose in the face of its potential undoing.

Anti-essentialist perspectives and an appreciation of the fictional quality of knowledge categories are not the only insights from late modern critical theory relevant to our problem. There is also, for example, the matter of marked and unmarked signifiers. What is political theory . . . today? To pursue the question without the temporal qualifier would be to eschew not only the contingency of identity production but its relentlessly historical quality. To pursue the question without the temporal qualifier is already to take a stance within the battle for political theory's future, one that aims for hegemony and refuses to avow its own dependencies and unconscious strategies. To let the temporal qualifier remain unspecified is also to propose to consider the nature and purpose of political theory in terms that disavow its historically constructed and contingent nature from the start, and thus to try to resurrect a truth undone by the enterprise of theory itself. So, then, what is political theory today . . . where? in the Anglo-American intellectual world? in western Europe or its eastern stepsibling? outside the metropoles of modernity? in the academy? in the streets? (whose streets?) To leave these matters unspecified is to remain blinkered to the long elite past of political theory as well as the saturation by colonial European and postwar American hegemony that has conditioned the identity and contents of recognized political theory in the more recent past. It is also to sustain, unreconstructed, the legacies of these pasts in the answer. And if we stipulate our question as "What is political theory today in the American academy?" we still need to ask about the work of that tiny verb, "is." Are we searching for the soul of an existing practice or a possible one? Are we asking what we do now, how we signify to others (which others?), or what we might become?[1] And if we are not forthrightly blending normative desire into description—if we really endeavor to describe our activity rather than our own particular investments in it—what sleights of hand are we engaged in then?

Still thinking about what contemporary critical theory might suggest about the question of "What is political theory," we learn from identity critique to inquire: What animates and invigorates this particular attempt to designate and distinguish a collective practice or way of life?

What might be feared or hoped for here that the stipulated identity is imagined to resolve or provide? If identity always entails a certain cessation in what Plato called "becoming," if it is always an attempt to consolidate being over becoming, if it is always a foreclosure of desire with ontology, of yearning with naming (of an "I want," in which the wanting incessantly deconstructs the I; with an "I am," in which the I fantasizes itself as immune to being undone by desire), of indeterminacy with a hardened list of attributes—if, in short, identity is always both a fall and a set of foreclosures, it may be instructive to attend to the anxieties or sufferings precipitating the call for identity resolution at this particular moment. What vulnerability to the inchoate, the impure, or the unknown appears to be untenable and in need of reprieve? What pressures on political theory to yield its boundaries or reach beyond itself appear radically imperiling to the enterprise and those working in its trenches?

Of course it is impossible, in a single essay, to take the measure of all that these questions open up, but we may nonetheless feel their disruptive presence as we pursue a narrower set of issues. One way to do this involves considering contemporary challenges to the identity of political theory through the frame of border politics. Which of modern Western academic political theory's constitutive borders are currently weakening or eroding, from what sources, and with what consequences for the enterprise? Where are these erosions producing fertile transformations of political theory's objects of study, self-understanding, and articulations with other disciplinary approaches? And where are these changes the occasion of a reactive identity formation—manifest either as anxious efforts to reconsolidate rapidly liquifying objects of analysis or as fierce policing of widening gaps in porous boundaries? And where might we see both transformative and reactive processes going on at once?

In what follows I will not consider every border or every strand of what has become an ornately subdivided field. I will not look closely, for example, at the changing boundary between philosophy and political theory organizing the territory and concerns of moral political thought, or that between new historicism and political theory configuring historicized interpretations of canonical works of theory. And I will not much consider the border between political theory and the discipline of political science, or political theory's particular and peculiar border with what has come to be denominated as formal theory. Certainly each of these could be the site of a productive inquiry. But I want to begin more broadly, with a set of late modern developments that have created substantial challenges for the particular strand of political theory addressed to contemporary political life and its possibilities, whether in a conserving, diagnostic, or prescriptive vein. These developments have historical-material wellsprings that in turn generate certain intellectual responses, both across academic thought and specifically within the profession of political theory. Provisionally and somewhat awkwardly, I will denote these late modern challenges to political theory as "world-historical," "intellectual," and "professional," and sketch each briefly.

WORLD HISTORY

World history, the ungainly term by which is signified the emergence of certain forces and the transformation of certain orders of existence that exceed any locally or nationally instigated events, offers a host of challenges to the boundedness and autonomy of politics. Here is how it goes today: nation-state sovereignty recedes while *economic* forces and transnational institutions come to the fore as major global actors; *culture* patently shapes political identity and drives political conflict and affiliation; *nature* emerges as an intensely agentic political force and politicized field, neither immune to human construction nor lacking a politics of its own; the *bodily*, the *ethnic*, and the *sexual* have erupted as dense sites of local, national, and international conflict; the *domestic* withers to its smallest possible dimensions and content, where it both is denaturalized by relentless commodification and erupts as a province of power saturated with relations of inegalitarianism, domination, and exploitation; the *social* or the *civic*, rather than the state, is increasingly figured as the domain of democracy—*social movement* is the name for popular political mobilization, and civil society is the designated sphere for political association, participation, and virtue (its absence is denoted as a "crisis" for democracy); and finally, historically specific *global* powers are understood to have diverse *local* effects, and hence the temporally contingent and the local become sites for theorizing and enacting democratic resistance to these powers.

These developments—whether regarded as effects of globalized capitalism or as effects of late modernity more broadly—are significant for political theory; indeed, they are almost (but not quite) deadly in their significance. With them, the traditional outcasts from the political as it has been widely conceived in Western political thought—economics, culture, nature, the bodily, the domestic, the social, the civic, and the local—come home to roost. In this return, they dilute the distinctiveness, the hypostasized purity of political theory, just as surely as the past half century's migration of the colonials to the metropoles has irreversibly undone the conceit of (pure) (European) Man. It is difficult to choose the most apt postcolonial metaphor here: have these phenomena forced an encounter with the inherent hybridity or impurity of the political, or have they disseminated and hence unbounded the political? or both? Perhaps different developments function differently, some producing hybrids, as in the fusion of certain cultural and political phenomena or the expansion of the politicized economy, while others figure the dissemination of the political (e.g., the construal of many facets of domestic life—from child care to domestic violence to the definition of marriage—as political and legal concerns). What is common within this variety is the potential identity crisis for political theory threatened by these developments. If, for example, democratic political life is increasingly understood as negotiated at temporally contingent and spatially local levels, what happens to the universal and transhistorical signature of political theory? If politics is in culture and culture is relentlessly political, what denotes the boundary between political theory and anthropological or other kinds of cultural theory, including theories of art, music, film? If the public/private distinction is in part ideological and functions to obscure the saturation of the private sphere by power and convention, then what is the difference between political theory and feminist theory devoted to theorizing this saturation? Indeed, what, other than anxiety about loss of identity and place, animates the drawing of a line between feminist theory and political theory, between theories of culture and theories of politics, between social or political economic theory and political theory? What remains of the *genre* of political theory other than an obvious and anxious power move to demote these other kinds of inquiry to subgeneric status? What would be the function of this move other than to preserve a realm itself undone by history?

Intellectual Migrations

The intellectual migrations effecting the boundaries around political theory are occasioned in part by the world-historical developments listed above but contain their own contingencies as well. The work of thinking about political matters theoretically has lately been under-taken in disciplines as far removed from each other and from political science as art history, anthropology, rhetoric, geography, and literature. To a degree, this is an effect of the late modern dissemination of the political described above; when culture appears to be suffused with politics, anthropologists and art historians inevitably become political theorists even as political theorists take up culture as an object of analysis. However, the intellectual dissemination of political theory beyond the bounds of philosophy and political science also issues from a consequential rethinking of *power* over the past half century.

In the nineteenth century, Marx challenged the boundaries of politi-cal theory with his discovery of power in the social—specifically, economic—realm. The blow this argument delivered to the line between political and social theory could be parried only by refusing Marx's in-sistence on the primacy of the economic, which was exactly Arendt's move; in a different vein, Foucault's; and of course the move of bour-geois liberals. In the past forty years, however, the disciplinary chal-lenge has come from another direction, one more difficult for political theory to repel because it concerns not merely the venue but the very conceptualization of what Weber called "the lifeblood of politics": power. Recent Continental thought—not only in philosophy but also in structuralist and poststructuralist linguistics, anthropology, semi-otics, literary theory, psychoanalysis, and history—has radically recon-ceived the operations, mechanics, circulation, logics, venues, and vehicles of power. On the one hand, power has been discerned in juxtapositions of images, relations between words, discourses of scien-tific truth, microorganizations of bodies and gestures, and social or-chestrations of pain and pleasure, sickness, fear, health, and suffering. On the other hand, these reconceptualizations have devastated con-ventional formulations of power—those that cast power as merely negative or repressive, as commodifiable and transferable, as inher-ently related to violence or to law. Understandings of power have also been transformed and enriched by work in feminist theory, postcolo-nial theory, critical race theory, and queer theory: no longer is it possi-ble to reduce stratification by gender, sexuality, race, or ethnicity to semiotic or biological essences on the one hand, or to mere effects of law, policy, or social prejudice on the other. Rather, as effects of power, these formations highlight the manifestation and circulation of power carried in imagistic and discursive representations, in psychic subjection, in spatial organization, in the disciplining of bodies and knowledges. They concretize the Derridean and Foucauldian insights into power's *normative* actions and effects. They make it difficult if not impossible to return to simple equations of power with sovereignty, rule, or wealth.

In addition to the reformulations of power discussed above, there is another matter concerning power that is now significant for political theory: namely, the status of capitalism in our thinking. For a number of reasons, capitalism is not much on political theory's agenda today. First and most important, it appears unchallengeable. Second, it is difficult to make the case for alternatives—either for their viability or for the possibility of achieving them. Third, over the past century and a half, in many ways capitalism has become steadily less odious for the majority populations of the First World; gone are the scenes of the masses laboring at starvation wages for the wealth of the few, except in the Third World. Capitalist commodity production is also ever more oriented to the pleasures of the middle-class consumer, and the middle class is ever more oriented by its own pleasures. Thus, writes Giorgio Agamben, "while the state in decline lets its empty shell survive everywhere as a pure structure of sovereignty and domination, society as a whole is . . . irrevocably delivered to the form of consumer society, that is, a society in which the sole goal of production is comfortable living."[2] Capitalism charms rather than alienates us with its constant modifications of our needs and with its output for our mere entertainment, and we are remarkably acclimated to its production of algorithmic increases in the rates of redundancy and replacement of technologies. Fourth, however cynically or superficially, First World capitalism has developed an ethical face: it recycles, conserves, and labels; it divests itself of genetically modified organisms and transfats, and caters to kosher, vegetarian, and heart-healthy diets; it refrains from testing on animals and develops dolphin-safe tuna nets; it donates fractions of its profits to cancer research and reforestation, and sponsors Special Olympics, gay pride, summer Bach festivals, and educational supplements for the underprivileged. Save for occasional revelations about heinous sweatshop practices or dire devastations of pristine nature, it has largely lost its brutish reputation as a ruthless exploiter and polluter. With the aid of the media that it also owns, it has effectively transferred this reputation to images of power-mongering, desperate, ignorant, or fundamentalist sites in the Third World—the Taliban, Castro, the People's Republic of China, the rubber tappers of the Brazilian rain forest. Fifth, these changes in capitalism itself are complemented by recent left intellectual tendencies that deflect attention from capitalism as a crucible of unfreedom and inegalitarianism. When the seeming perdurability of capitalism, the absence of compelling alternatives, capitalism's devotion to consumer pleasures, and its ostensibly improved conscience are combined with increased theoretical attention to other orders of injustice—those highlighted by multiculturalist or identify politics—capitalism slips into the background as an object of critique or political concern. Sixth, the rise of professionalism (about which more below) in political theory, and the apolitical nature of much theory and theoretical exchange, means that this movement into the background goes largely uncontested even by those who consider themselves to be on the cultural left. Finally, the repair of most Marxists to their own journals and conferences (this, too, a symptom of professionalism), and the extent to which many Anglo-American Marxists have substituted "postmodernism" and "identity politics" for capitalism as the chief target of their wrath and analytical attention, means that the Marxist project of illuminating the place of capitalism in political and social life has pretty much vanished from the orbit of political theory.

Yet if capitalism has all but disappeared as a subject and object of political theory (notwithstanding routine drive-by references to "globalization"), capitalism is and remains our life form. Understood not just as a mode of production, distribution, or exchange but as an unparalleled maker of history, capital arguably remains the dominant force in the organization of collective human existence, conditioning every element of social, political, cultural, intellectual, emotional, and kin life. Indeed, what for Marx constituted the basis for a critique of capital deeper than its exploitation and denigration of labor, deeper than the disparities between wealth and poverty it organized, is that capital is a larger, more creative, and more nearly total form of power than anything else in human history, yet it fundamentally escapes human control. In Marx's view, this unparalleled power, and not merely its inegalitarian distribution of wealth was what rendered capital such a profoundly antidemocratic historical force: too little is ours to craft or control as long as this force organizes and produces our world; too little can be ordered according to democratic deliberation about human need, gratification, or enhancement—not our work, our values, our fortunes, our enmities, our modes of education, our styles of love, or the content of our suffering. This is not to say that capital is the only significant social power afoot in the contemporary world. We have learned otherwise from Nietzsche, Freud, Weber, du Bois, de Beauvoir, Fanon, Foucault, and their respective contemporary heirs. Yet while it is importantly supplemented by these teachings, Marx's insight into capital's awesome power to shape both human history and agentic possibility is not diminished by them.

No one could have predicted how the force of this insight would intensify between Marx's time and the present. Our problem today, however, is less with its intensification than with what to do with it when both the science of history and the revolutionary impulse that Marx counted on have collapsed, when the validity of the critique persists but there appears nothing to be done about it. For Marx, the depth of the critique was matched by the depth and reach of the redemptive promise. Today this promise is very nearly extinguished. That the most powerful undemocratic force in human history appears to be here to stay—this is the fundamental left and liberal predicament today, a predicament that haunts our theoretical and political practices concerned with freedom, equality, justice, and more.

This haunting is not the only consequence of failing to engage the powers of capitalism in our work. Rather, our averted glance here also prevents us from grasping the extent to which the dramatic alterations in the configuration of the political discussed under the rubric of "world history" are themselves effects of capitalism, and not simply of secularization, disenchantment, or contingent human invention. To paraphrase from the *Communist Manifesto*, capitalism is a world-class boundary smasher—there is nothing it cannot penetrate, infiltrate, rearrange, hybridize, commodify, invent, dissolve. The movement of capital is largely responsible for the extent to which boundaries have been erased, in late modernity, between activities or spheres historically bearing at least a modest distinction from one another in terms of space, style, organization, or function, including the university and the corporation, sex and technology, and the political and the cultural. Thus, to theorize the politics of recognition, the sexual order of things, the nature of citizenship, or the reconfiguration of privacy without taking the measure of their historically specific production *by* capitalism is literally not to know the constitutive conditions of one's object of analysis. It is not to be able to grasp the powers organizing life in our time and hence to risk ontologizing this organization and reifying its effects. Finally, to the degree that potential transformations are figured in abstraction from the powers delimiting possibility, it is to make political theory into fantasy play.

PROFESSIONALIZATION

> Political theory might be defined in general terms as a tradition of
> discourse concerned about the present being and well-being of
> collectivities. It is primarily a civic and secondarily an academic
> activity. In my understanding this means that political theory is a
> critical engagement with collective existence and with the
> political experiences of power to which it gives rise.
> —SHELDON WOLIN, *The Presence of the Past*

The practice of political theory has probably never been as profession-
alized as it is today, a phenomenon certainly shaped by external forces
but heartily taken up from within political theory's ranks, and even by
the most young and hip among its ranks. By *professionalization*, I mean
in part the organization of a practice whose referent is itself, whose audience and judges are one another, and whose existence is tallied and
certified by conferences, journals, prizes, recruitments, and other
markers of recognition conferred according to established hierarchies
and norms. I also mean the orientation of those within the profession
to these markers, and the setting of an agenda of inquiry by them.

The Oxford English Dictionary provides a fuller sense of the pejorative
implications of professionalization. A profession is, broadly, "any calling or occupation by which a person habitually earns his living," but
the term appears to derive from that aspect of the word *profess* referring
to "the declaration, promise, or vow made by one entering a religious
order; hence, the action of entering such an order." Moreover, as Weber
emphasized in his essays on politics and science as vocations, the professional is not simply distinguished by degree of expertise in relation
to the amateur, but is one who, in the words of the *OED*, "makes a profession or business of any occupation, art, or sport, otherwise usually
or often engaged in by amateurs, esp. as a pasttime." Thus, the dictionary notes, *professional* is a term "disparagingly applied to one who
'makes a trade' of anything that is properly pursued from higher
motives, as a *professional politician*." The notions of entry into a religious
order, with all the oaths, vows, hierarchy, norms, and gatekeeping that
such entry entails, and of the conversion of an intrinsically worthy endeavor into an instrument of personal or financial gain together give
some indication of what may be at stake and especially what may be
the costs of the growing professionalization of political theory.

Most severe among these costs is the steady attenuation of political theory's orientation both to political life and to politically interested intellectuals outside the discipline. Debates within the profession are more often framed by internal quarrels—communitarian versus liberal, Habermas versus Foucault—than by problems or events in the political world, and the value of our contributions to these debates is mediated by degrees of recognition within the profession, a mediation whose outcome is largely predetermined by established hierarchies and networks. We are thus vulnerable to the very charge most often leveled against our most methodologically oriented political science colleagues: explanatory or normative power in the political world is rarely the referent for our work or the index of its worth.

The growing balkanization of political theory, and a relative sanguinity among political theorists about this balkanization, can also be understood in terms of the forces of professionalization.[3] If professional recognition for a particular kind of work is scarce or unavailable in one subcaste of political theory, then it is easy enough to declare a new field or new juxtaposition of fields, anthologize a group of theorists in this area, inaugurate a new journal or professional association, or found a new American Political Science Association section. Ironically, such breakaway efforts, which are themselves the effects of professionalism, are often misrecognized by those who undertake them as antiprofessional political projects, with the consequence that the work of building a new institutional and intellectual niche in the profession is framed as struggle in the front lines of a real-world political skirmish. Of course knowledge is always political and politics always involves battles over knowledge claims, but the stakes of these narrow professional battles (predominantly but not exclusively matters of employment, advancement, and above all signification within and recognition by a minuscule readership) surely do not exhaust the possibilities for political theory's articulation with political life.

The current professionalization of political theory is overdetermined. It is configured in part by contemporary pressures to professionalize and commodify every vocation, indeed every pasttime, no matter how countercultural (think of the "professional" skateboarder, rapper, or body-piercing artist), and by the corporatization of every aspect of public and private enterprise, including the university. But if these were its only sources, at least some political theorists—those who consider themselves opposed to the commodification and corporatization of everyday life—would be more likely to resist than to abet the process. Yet the rarity of such resistance raises the question of whether professionalization serves as a bulwark against felt worldly impotence on the one hand, and against identity erosion and loss of secure territory for political theorists on the other—in short, as partial insulation against some of the boundary-eroding, identity-dissolving forces of the world-historical and intellectual terrain shifts discussed above.

Our political world today is full of power, forces, and events, but rather short on collective action. There are exceptions, of course—the Velvet Revolution, Tiananmen Square, even World Trade Organization protests—but as suggested in the discussion of capitalism above, the contemporary political world is largely organized by enormous forces and institutions controlled by no one and immensely difficult to challenge. We live this paradox daily in small and large ways: the world is radically disenchanted and, at the same time, the metaforces structuring it, the metadynamics moving it, are in no one's hands and (*pace* Marx) stand little chance of coming under individual or collective human command. This does not necessarily complicate the work of political critique and diagnosis, but it severely problematizes the aspect of critical political theory oriented to the question "What is to be done?" For those who insist on a tight, even seamless connection between diagnosis and action, who require that the action remedy the illness as defined by the theory, the situation becomes especially thorny: a political world immune to large-scale augmentation by human action is a world inevitably frustrating to critical political theorists. And so we take flight: into moral theory, which mostly works in abstraction from the concrete powers organizing political life; into ethics and aesthetics, in which relations with the other and with the world are generally theorized without strong reference to contemporary orders of power; into an ironic *amor fati* extended toward the world; or into pure critique. Or we simply retreat into the profession, where impassioned arguments and position taking need not resonate with the contemporary political landscape.

A second phenomenon weakening resistance to professionalization pertains to the boundary erosion in intellectual life discussed above. That the boundaries around political theory appear particularly porous and contestable today is a problem not only for the identity of the field but for the identity of individual political theorists. If a scholar of English literature writes brilliantly on Hobbes's *Leviathan*, if cultural anthropologists are currently the most incisive theorists of nationalism, if scholars of gender and race have developed genuinely new perspectives on social contract theory, if geographers have some of the most astute insights into the political implications of the transformations of time and space wrought by post-Fordist capitalism, then who am I and who is my constituency or reading audience? Indeed, if the disciplinary boundaries really disintegrate, what obscurity lies in wait for us in a world much vaster than a small cadre of colleagues whose card of entry to the order is modest mastery of approximately two dozen great books and fluency with a small number of watchwords: justice, liberty, power, obligation, constitutions, equality, citizenship, action, government, rule, polity? And what better way to secure ourselves against this impending identity crisis and potential obscurity than to resort to ever more public, organized, and policed recognition and certification of who and what we are?

I want to consider now these three domains in which political theory's boundaries are negotiated—the domain of the world, the domain of intellectual life, and the domain of the profession—as harboring three different forces exerted on and in the field of political theory. The world-historical developments I have outlined are primarily *dispersive* in their effect on our subject matter; they corrode the boundaries between zones of human existence that have historically produced the ontological autonomy of the political and thus disperse the political itself. The intellectual developments, especially by disturbing conventional formulations of power and contesting conventional locales of power, *disseminate* the currency of the field and also parallel the world-historical effects by *dispelling* the boundaries historically constitutive of its epistemological autonomy. The professionalizing tendencies, while engaging some of these effects, mostly run in the opposite direction, *constricting and narrowing* the reach of the field and its qualified participants. In addition, professionalization invariably entails a turn away from the political world and even from a potential intellectual audience for political theory outside of its own membership. In short, we have on the one hand dispersive, disseminating, and dispelling forces, and, on the other, a constricting and containing force.

A vibrant future for political theory depends in part on developing *contrapuntal* strategies in engaging the three sets of forces contouring and agitating its boundaries. Why counterpoint? Late modernity has revealed the limits in most of the usual models for holding together two or more truths. The many inflections of *dialectic* bear a common dependence on a magically metaphysical meeting of opposites, indeed a construction of the formulations at stake *as* opposites, and also often a dependence on a progressive metanarrative. Though *paradox* tends to be anti-political in the mutual undoing (by virtue of multiplicity) of the truths it addresses, *contradiction*, figuring mutual cancellation, tends to be forthrightly paralyzing. Psychic models of an opposition between *conscious* and *unconscious* truths forecast either eruptive acting out or therapeutic adjustment (or resignation), as opposed to political generativity. *Pluralism* capitulates to relativism and celebrates the incommensurability of multiple truths without giving us a clue about how to weigh or navigate them. *Integration* always entails the high price of assimilation; invariably, one side normatively governs and incorporates the other, which then must cede a part of itself. And *irony* mainly grimaces—comically or tragically—at the loss of truth sustained by multiplying or removing grounds or accountability from truth claims.

In addition to coming up short in epistemological viability or political generativity, each of these models involves submitting one truth to the other. None provides a frame in which several truths are enriched even as they are offset by each other . . . or better, a frame in which the relation or even interlocution between two truths enriches each, offsetting to set off or incite one another. Moreover, none allows the truths themselves to be dynamic and the proliferation of truth itself to be part of the dynamism. So I want to borrow from the arts, and especially music, another way of holding things together: namely counterpoint, a deliberate practice of multiplicity that exceeds simple opposition and does not carry the mythological or methodological valence of dialectics or contradiction. At once open-ended and tactical, counterpoint emanates from and promotes an antihegemonic sensibility and requires a modest and carefully styled embrace of multiplicity in which contrasting elements, featured simultaneously, do not simply war, harmonize, blend, or compete but rather bring out complexity that cannot emerge through a monolithic or single melody. This complexity does not add up to a whole but rather sets off a theme by providing it an elsewhere; indeed, it can even highlight and thus contest dominance through its work of juxtaposition.

Whether in music, painting, or verbal argument, counterpoint first complicates a single or dominant theme through the addition of contrasting themes or forces; it undoes a monolithic element through the multiplication of elements. Second, counterpoint sets off or articulates a thematic by means of contrast or juxtaposition; it highlights dominance through a kind of reverse othering. Both of these moves are useful for the multifold project of renewing political theory's political concerns, renovating its identity, and developing its capacity to intervene in the restructuring of intellectual life. Together they figure a late modern strategy for bringing to light and resisting certain forces that otherwise shape our practices. Here are some of the ways this contrapuntal strategy might work.

It is crucial that political theorists learn to move and work in the larger and less clearly demarcated, disciplined, and territorialized fields of thought and existence opened by recent world-history and intellectual redistricting. Yet if political theory is concerned with the human negotiation of the powers, governance, and values of collective life, then it remains our task to discern and cultivate the distinctive spaces and idioms in which such negotiation can occur. This means, I think, taking the measure of the recent world historical and intellectual dispersion and dissemination of the political without simply capitulating to it, naively celebrating it, or abetting it. Indeed, it means drawing (nonabsolute) distinctions on behalf of distinctively political life and doing so against the very historical tide that is washing them away. In part an intervention in the political and intellectual world, a potential renewal of our identity as political theorists also occurs in this coming to terms with the contemporary conditions of political life and political theory and in self-consciously cultivating agency and identity from within these conditions.

Let me try to introduce more precision here. If the political is signaled by the presence of any human relations organized by power, which is one important way to signal it (especially if one seeks to demystify or denaturalize a particular order of domination), than it is inevitable that we would find the political everywhere today—in cultural, familial, economic, and psychosexual relations, and more. But if the political is alternatively signaled by the distinct problematic of negotiating the powers and values of enduring collectivities, which is another important way to signal it (especially if one seeks to attend to the prospects for democracy in late modernity), then the political cannot simply be indicated by the presence of power.[4] The intellectual tendencies of the past quarter century have been toward the first formulation, while conventional political theory clings hard to the second. The first renders almost everything political (and renders all theory political theory);

the second radically delimits the scope of the political, and tends not to see the politicalness of many of its own predicates—knowledge, language, kinship, nature, gender, regulatory norms, and more. What if we were to tack between these perspectives, retaining the emphasis on collectivity while expanding our sense of the reach and operations of power that collectivities harbor and through which collective life can be studied—the complex subjects and subjectivities, the rich range of discourses and practices constituting them?

We can approach the same problem through the phenomenon of politicization and the dissemination of the problem of power in late modernity. To speak of politicizing something generally carries one of two meanings: either it entails corrupting a process or domain of activity with issues of interest or advantage, as in "The job search became so politicized that hiring the best candidate wasn't even a possibility," or it involves revealing relations of power in something ordinarily conceived in other terms, as in "Feminist theory has politicized gender, showing it to be an effect of power rather than a natural phenomenon." What is common to these seemingly disparate usages is that politicization introduces power where it was presumed not to exist before. But in the wake of late-twentieth-century thought, especially Foucault, we now know power to be everywhere in the human universe, which means that, quite literally, everything pertaining to human existence can be politicized. Does this make everything pertaining to human existence the subject of political theory? (Does Plato triumph after all?) It is this move that I am counseling against, suggesting instead that we carve a distinction between the politicization of particular relations and endeavors, such as science or canon formation or sex, and the bearing of this politicization on the political where the latter is understood as the distinct problematic of the values and powers binding collectivities. This is not to say that politicization is irrelevant to the political—far from it. As Marx politicized private property, as feminists and gay activists have politicized marriage, so an understanding of the exclusions and injuries performed by depoliticized forms of domination or regulation—those shrouded in discourses of the natural or the neutral—is crucial material for political theorists. But theoretical politicization of any activity or relation is not the same as theorizing the political, just as the presence of power, *precisely because it is everywhere*, cannot be equated with the problem of how we do and ought to order collective life.

Though the world-historical and intellectual disseminations of the political may be simultaneously thematized and offset by a self-conscious and strategic re-territorialization of the political on the part of political theory, the conservative, narrowing, and constraining effects of professionalism on political theory require a different kind of counterpoint. Here, deliberate and careful transgression, risk, and interdisciplinary adventurousness are in order—these are the strategies that will facilitate erudition in the organizing features of our time, and make us worldly rather than narrow in our political theoretical approach to them. These are also the strategies that will educate us in the characteristics of language and rhetoric, and in the techniques of reading and thinking, that have been developed so richly outside the discipline and are essential to our work. It is here, in our choice of research materials, colleagues, and audience, that we can most artfully confront the identity dissolution of political theory incited by the disseminating effects of the world-historical and intellectual configurations of our time. It is here that we may most productively consort with those who are not our kind—those from other fields and with other foci—and not only be stretched by but also recover a sense of the project of political theory through this encounter.

Political theory aimed at critically apprehending our contemporary condition, I am suggesting, needs to closely engage but not surrender to the contemporary disseminations of politics, power, and theory. Our historically constitutive terms and questions—about power, action, political institutions, freedom, stability, change, membership, equality, obligation, domination, and justice—will indubitably continue to organize our work and identity, even as other terms are added. But while we allow these terms and questions to be reconfigured by the world-historical changes and the intellectual developments that have so dramatically altered their meanings from what they were a century or twenty-five centuries ago, we can also reassert the singular value of political theory by recovering our constitutive orientation to the problem of how collectivities are conceived and ordered in the contemporary world, a world that poses as a most urgent and open question what kinds of collectivities currently or will next order and contain humanity. Thus, issues of rule, sovereignty, and legitimacy, which persist as important problems, will contend on the one side with the loss of stable sovereign entities—states or subjects—and on the other with the discovery of other orders of power that rival sovereignty in the ordering of collectivities. Questions about justice, our founding and enduring question, cannot presume a temporally stable, transcendental, and undifferentiated concept of man; cannot presume the cultural neutrality of liberal (or any other) values; cannot elide economic, familial, sexual, gendered, or racial orders of power that bear on what is just. Questions about the nature of the political cannot presume its radical independence from the cultural, the economic, and, above all, the technological. Questions about the relation of public and private must take the measure of the "politics" discovered in the private realm by a quarter century of feminist theory, of the complex hybridizations of public and private produced by contemporary capitalism, and, of course, of the fantastic reconfigurations of the meaning and experience of public and private induced by contemporary digital technologies. Questions about membership and citizenship will take the measure of the unstable, composite, dynamic, and often incoherent nature of contemporary collectivities at the international, national, and subnational level; they must grapple with the slackening of the state-citizen tie and the awkward, multiple, and often fractious nature of other, especially transnational, claims on membership and forces of subjection, fealty, or obligation. Can citizenship be thought apart from generations-long belonging to a stable nation-state and hence independently of state sovereignty, law, constitutions, or ethnic-religious homogeneity? What genealogical rupture in the mutually constitutive state-citizen relation does this thought require?

As I have suggested, political theory (or political science, for that matter) is not the field that has most knowledgeably, carefully, or artfully explored the late modern transmogrifications in the configurations of social, political, economic, and cultural life invoked in the formulations above, any more than it is the field that has developed the richest understandings of language, interpretation, and argument.[5] Although some contemporary political theory nods to the charred ground of conventional citizenship in its attempt to theorize "culture," "group rights," "difference," and "language," for example, much contemporary theorizing about citizenship remains linked to social contractarian accounts of the state, society, and individual on one side, or to attempts to move liberal principles of individualism and altruism toward an abstract cosmopolitanism or "parallel polis" on the other. Certainly, there is no need for political theorists to conduct primary research on the restructuring entailed in globalization; but in order to theorize the implications of this restructuring, we must go to the work that exhumes and examines it—in anthropology, cultural studies, political economy, geography, media studies. As political theorists, we do not need to develop original theories of rhetoric, semiotics, or interpretation; but in order to be effective readers of texts—events, canonical works, or historical developments—and in order to be as rigorous and self-reflexive as possible in the construction of our own arguments, we need to consult the fields that do undertake these studies, especially literary, rhetorical, and visual theory. If we do not make these crossings, we literally make ourselves stupid . . . about this world and the knowledges that will incisively apprehend and criticize it. This imperative, of course, also renders our contemporary task enormous, requiring as it does an expanded erudition that is wide and not only deep.

But this interdisciplinary traveling is only one antidote for the condition of political theory today, a combination of theoretical and historical conservatism, hyperprofessionalism, and a certain remoteness from the world. If we are to survive the current erosions of our identity with more than a profession intact, we also need to introduce counterpoint to the anti-political tendencies of professionalism. Doing so would involve cultivating a political orientation for our work and thus foregrounding concern with the question of how collective life is ordered, what powers and possibilities it harbors, and what prospects exist for advancing the values we argue that it should feature. No matter how much boundary crossing we do at the level of knowledge, it is only this turn that will renew the identity of political theory amid current challenges. Such a turn not only implies replacing professionalism with the political world for sources of incitement and even a potential audience, it also involves close theoretical engagement with the powers now organizing political life, especially those of capitalism, with which I have suggested contemporary political theory has often been disinclined to engage.

But in this effort to reverse political theory's retreat into professionalism and to reorient it toward politics, if the future of political theory is to approximate or even carry a trace of the richness of its past, we must also beware of capitulating to a certain pressure on theory itself today—to apply, to be True, or to solve immediate real-world problems. This pressure has several sources, but the current "information phase" of capital is crucial: as information itself is unprecedentedly commodified and at the same time becomes the most significant commodity, this commodification and this significance effectively diminish the value of all thought not readily commodified. Hence the intensifying demand on and in the universities, even on the humanities and arts, for knowledge that is applicable and marketable. Such expectations, combined with steadily growing corporate sponsorship of university life, overtly and indirectly incite us to turn against the autonomous value of theory; consciously and unconsciously, we are threatened with a terrifying degree of academic marginalization, perhaps even extinction, if we submit theory to this emerging table of values.

Why can't theory meet the demand for applicability or usefulness without being sacrificed? What is it about theory that is destroyed by such a demand? The question of theory's nature and purview today is fiercely contested; even as a question, it is markedly fragmented—no two disciplines or subfields mean the same thing by theory or value it in the same way.[6] Within political science alone, the appellation of *theory* has been appropriated for an extraordinary range of work—from rational choice and game theory to cultural and literary theory to analytic philosophy to hermeneutics to historical interpretations of canonical works. But in all cases, just as politics and political theory define themselves against and through their hypothesized others, so too theory takes its definition through differentiation, whether from empiricism, method, science, storytelling, the arts, history, Truth, experience, poetry, or observation. That these alterities are what create and circumscribe theory is not the problem. Instead, it is a contemporary anxiety about theory's difference as such, and in particular about its enigmatic and otherworldly character, that we would do well to allay rather than submit to.

Theory is not simply different from description; rather, it is incommensurate with description.[7] Theory is not simply the opposite of application but carries the impossibility of application. As a meaning-making enterprise, theory depicts a world that does not quite exist, that is not quite the world we inhabit. But this is theory's incomparable value, not its failure. Theory does not simply decipher the meanings of the world but recodes and rearranges them in order to reveal something about the meanings and incoherencies that we live with. To do this revelatory and speculative work, theory must work to one side of direct referents, or at least it must disregard the conventional meanings and locations of those referents. Theory violates the self-representation of things in order to represent those things and their relation—the world—differently. Thus, theory is never "accurate" or "wrong"; it is only more or less illuminating, more or less provocative, more or less of an incitement to thought, imagination, desire, possibilities for renewal.

There is another reason that theory cannot be brought to the bar of truth or applicability. Insofar as theory imbues contingent or unconscious events, phenomena, or formations with meaning and with location in a world of theoretical meaning, theory is a sense-making enterprise of that which often makes no sense, of that which may be inchoate, unsystematized, inarticulate. It gives presence to what may have a liminal, evanescent, or ghostly existence. Thus theory has no kinship with the project of "accurate representation"; its value lies instead in the production of a new representation, in the production of coherence and meaning that it does not find lying on the ground but which, rather, it forthrightly fashions. Similarly, theory does not simply articulate needs or desires but argues for their existence and thus literally brings them into being. As theory interprets the world, it fabricates that world (*pace* Marx! especially Marx!); as it names desire, it gives reason and voice to desire, and thus fashions a new order of desire; as it codifies meaning, it composes meaning. Theory's most important *political* offering is this opening of a breathing space between the world of common meanings and the world of alternative ones, a space of potential renewal for thought, desire, and action. And it is this which we sacrifice in capitulating to the demand that theory reveal truth, deliver applications, or solve each of the problems it defines. In responding to the pressures of professionalism, then, a double counterpoint is needed to counter the deflection of political theory's attention from contemporary political life and its anxiety about its "difference" from other modes of inquiry—its remove from the empirical, from facticity, from accurate representation, from Truth. While perhaps contradictory at first blush, the projects of retrieving the world as an object of theory and of recovering the value of theory as a distinctive form of figuring the world not only both resist current troubling influences on the discipline but are also compatible in the attempt to renew the identity of political theory: they connect our work to political theory's rich canonical past while honing it for the work of understanding a singular present.

Political theory, in addition to losing many of its territory markers in recent decades, has tacitly ceded sovereignty over its own subject matter. This condition, I have suggested, is the consequence of (1) a dissemination of power and politics, a dissemination about which political theory must become erudite *and* in which it must intervene; (2) political theory's relative failure to be enriched by interpretive and rhetorical techniques developed elsewhere in the humanities and

interpretive social sciences; (3) political theory's attenuated relation to
the subject of political life understood as the negotiation of power in
collectivities; and (4) challenges to theory's intrinsic worth that press it
in the direction of applied social science. Recovery of our identity in
the face of disseminated theories and practices of politics hinges on recovery of our value. Recovery of our value in turn depends on the acquisition of fluency in the complexities of power and language as they
have been elaborated outside the discipline; it depends as well on
cutting across currents of professionalism in order to draw our questions and cares from political life, broadly construed, and in order at
least partially to insulate theory from the relentless commodification
and capitalization of knowledge. A tall order? It is possible that the
human world has never been so difficult to fathom, to theorize, to
imagine justice for, to render just. Our theoretical blankets of comfort
have perhaps never been thinner, nor the promise of redemption more
faint. We should not be astonished that our work is so hard.

FIVE

■　■　■

FREEDOM'S SILENCES

HEGEL rendered philosophical what the ancient Athenian elites had struggled with existentially and tragically: if freedom inheres in the capacity to choose a course of action, then it is simultaneously realized and negated in the very act of choosing. Commitment to a particular course of action forecloses the freedom that enabled the commitment. In this regard, freedom is not merely paradoxical in its workings but self-canceling and, finally, unachievable. Hence Foucault's warning that freedom lies neither in institutions nor in ideals and proclamations, but only in practices.

As freedom is both realized and negated by choice, so is silence convened, broken, and organized by speech. Silence and speech are not only constitutive of but also modalities of one another. They are different kinds of articulation that produce as well as negate each other. Silence calls for speech, yet speech, because it is always particular speech, vanquishes other possible speech, thus canceling the promise of full representation heralded by silence. Silence, both constituted and broken by particular speech, is neither more nor less "truthful" than speech is, and neither more nor less regulatory. Speech harbors silences; silences harbor meaning. When silence is broken by speech, new silences are fabricated and enforced; when speech ends, the ensuing silence carries meaning that can only be metaphorized by speech, thus producing the conviction that silence speaks.

The belief that silence and speech are opposites is a conceit underlying most contemporary discourse about censorship and silence. This conceit enables both the assumption that censorship converts the truth of speech to the lie of silence and the assumption that when an enforced silence is broken, what emerges is truth borne by the vessel of authenticity or experience. Calling these assumptions into question means not only thinking about the relation between silence and speech differently but also rethinking the powers and potentials of silence.

Here is the way this problem unfolds politically: insurrection requires breaking silence about the very existence as well as the activity or injury of the collective insurrectionary subject. Even dreams of emancipation cannot take shape unless the discursively shadowy or altogether invisible character of those subjects, wounds, events, or activities is redressed, whether through slave ballads, the flaunting of forbidden love, the labor theory of value, or the quantification of housework. Nor are the silences constituted in discourses of subordination broken forever when they are broken once. They do not shatter the moment their strategic function has been exposed, but must be assaulted repeatedly with stories, histories, theories, and discourses in alternate registers until the silence itself is rendered routinely intelligible as a historically injurious force. In this way, those historically excluded from liberal personhood have proceeded against the spectrum of silences limning the universal claims of humanist discourse for the past several centuries. Jews, immigrants, women, people of color, homosexuals, the unpropertied: all have pressed themselves into civic belonging not simply through asserting their personhood but through politicizing—articulating—the silent workings of their internally excluded presence within prevailing notions of personhood.

But while the silences in discourses of domination are a site for insurrectionary noise, while they are the corridors to be filled with explosive counter tales, it is also possible to make a fetish of breaking silence. It is possible as well that this ostensible tool of emancipation carries its own techniques of subjugation—that it converges with unemancipatory tendencies in contemporary culture, establishes regulatory norms, coincides with the disciplinary power of ubiquitous confessional practices; in short, it may feed the powers it meant to starve.

Neither a defense of silence nor an injunction to silence, this essay interrogates the presumed authenticity of "voice" in the implicit equation between speech and freedom entailed in contemporary affirmations of breaking silence. Borrowing tacitly from Foucault's theorization of confessional discourse, Joan W. Scott's problematization of experience, and Shoshana Felman's and Dori Laub's identification of our time as the age of testimony,[1] the essay asks whether our contemporary crisis of truth has not been displaced into an endless stream of words about ourselves, words that presume to escape epistemological challenges to truth because they are personal or experiential. It asks as well whether this stream of words does not perpetuate the crisis of which it is a symptom.

In the course of this inquiry, silence is considered as not simply an aesthetic but a political value, a means of preserving certain practices and dimensions of existence from regulatory power, from normative violence, as well as from the scorching rays of public exposure. A link is examined, too, between, on the one hand, a contemporary tendency concerning the lives of public figures—the confession or extraction of every detail (sexual, familial, therapeutic, financial) of private and personal life—and, on the other, a putatively countercultural or emancipatory practice: the compulsive putting into public discourse of heretofore hidden or private experiences, from catalogues of sexual pleasures to litanies of sexual abuses, from chronicles of eating disorders to diaries of home births and gay parenting. In linking these two phenomena—the privatization of public life via the mechanism of public exposure of private life on the one hand, and the compulsive and compulsory cataloguing of the details of marginalized lives on the other—I want to highlight a modality of regulation and depoliticization specific to our age that is not simply confessional but empties private life into the public domain. The effect is both to abet the steady commercialization and homogenization of intimate attachments, experiences, and emotions already achieved by the market and to usurp public space with often trivial matters, rendering the political personal in a fashion that leaves injurious social, political, and economic powers unremarked and untouched. In short, while intended as a practice of freedom (premised on the modernist conceit that the truth makes us free), these productions of truth may have the capacity not only to chain us to our injurious histories as well as the stations of our small lives, but to instigate the further regulation of those lives while depoliticizing their conditions.

My concern with what might be called compulsory discursivity and the presumed evil of silences has yet another source. Notwithstanding the engagement with Foucault by many intellectuals invested in contemporary progressive social movements, there is an oddly non- or pre-Foucauldian quality to much left and liberal debate about censorship and silencing. Expression is cast either as that which makes us free, tells "our" truth, and puts our truth into circulation, *or* as that which oppresses us by featuring "their" truth in the form of pornography, hate speech, harassment, or the representation of the world from "the male point of view."[2] Though one side in the debate argues for more expression on our part—for example, by making our own porn or telling our own stories—and the other argues for less on "their" part, both sides nonetheless subscribe to an *expressive* and *repressive* notion of speech, agreeing on its capacity to express the truth of an individual's desire or condition, or to repress that truth. Both equate freedom with voice and visibility, both assume recognition to be unproblematic when we tell our own story, and both assume that such recognition is the material of power as well as pleasure.[3] Neither confronts the regulatory potential in speaking ourselves, its capacity to bind rather than emancipate us.[4]

To inaugurate an analysis of the relationship between silence, speech, and freedom that questions the conventional discursive order in which they appear, I want to reflect on several passages from Foucault's work. The first is from *The History of Sexuality*:

> Discourses are not once and for all subservient to power or raised up against it, any more than silences are. . . . Discourse transmits and produces power; it reinforces it, but also undermines and exposes it, renders it fragile and makes it possible to thwart it. In like manner, silence and secrecy are a shelter for power, anchoring its prohibitions; but they also loosen its hold and provide for relatively obscure areas of tolerance.[5]

Foucault here marks the ambiguity of silence in relationship to power, insisting that silence functions not only as a "shelter *for* power" but also as a shelter *from* it. Foucault's example is the putative freedom of homosexual practice in a historical age when there is no formal discourse for or about it: "the nearly universal reticence in talking about [sodomy] made possible a twofold operation: . . . an extreme severity . . . and a [widespread] tolerance."[6] This understanding of the ambivalent "freedom" contained in the silence or "secret" of homosexuality is corroborated by Agnes Lugo-Ortiz's work on orality, law, and silence in the making of the Puerto Rican homosexual body, and by M. Jacqui Alexander's tracing of the production of "lesbian" as a category (heretofore unmarked in law) by the 1986 Sexual Offences Bill of Trinidad and Tobago.[7] Albeit quite differently, each reflects on the extent to which a silence "broken" by the production of a new public or institutional discourse may bring otherness *violently* into being as it brings a designated subject respectively into abjection, censure, or regulation. In Lugo-Ortiz's words, "through orality, a community that aspires to a totalizing self-definition exercises its law and its violence. Silence, in this case, may then be read as a radical deconstructive proposition against any pretense to political absolutism."[8] In the debate over the Sexual Offences Bill that is the subject of Alexander's study, lesbian sexuality emerges into public discourse in Trinidad and Tobago only for purposes of stigmatizing and criminalizing it, as part of the criminalization of all extramarital and nonreproductive sexual practices. What each case makes clear is that while to be invisible within a local discourse may occasion the injuries of social liminality, such suffering may be mild compared to that of radical denunciation, hystericization, exclusion, or criminalization.

The paradoxical capacity of silence to engage opposites with regard to power—both to shelter power and to serve as a barrier against power—is rarely accented in Foucault's thinking as a consequence of his emphasis (elsewhere) on discourse as a vehicle of power. In casting silence as a potential refuge from power, I do not think he is reneging on this emphasis or suggesting a prediscursive existence to things. Critical here is the difference between what Foucault calls *unitary* discourses, which regulate and colonize, and those that do not perform these functions with the same social pervasiveness, even while they do not escape the tendency of all discourse to establish norms by which it regulates and excludes. Through this distinction one can make sense of Foucault's otherwise inexplicable reference to sex in the eighteenth century as being "driven out of hiding and constrained to lead a discursive existence," or his troubling example of the village simpleton whose "inconsequential" sexual game with a little girl was suddenly subjected to medical, judicial, and popular scrutiny and condemnation.[9] Neither in these cases nor in others where Foucault seems to imply a "freer," because prediscursive, existence to certain practices does he appear to mean that they really occurred "outside" discourse; the point is rather that they had not yet been brought into the pervasive disciplinary or biopolitical discourses of the age—science, psychiatry, medicine, law, pedagogy.[10] Silence, as Foucault affirms it, is then identical neither with secrecy nor with not speaking. It instead signifies a particular relation to regulatory discourses, as well as a possible niche for the practice of freedom *within* those discourses.

Put differently, if discourses posit and organize silences, then silences themselves must be understood as discursively produced, as part of discourse, rather than as its opposite. Hence silences are no more free of organization by power than speech is, nor are they any more inventable or protectable by us than speech is. Yet, and paradoxically, silence—even that produced within discourse—may also function as that which discourse has not penetrated, as a scene of practices that escape the regulatory functions of discourse. It is this latter function that renders silence itself a source of protection and potentially even a source of power. The Fifth Amendment to the U.S. Constitution may be understood as mobilizing precisely this power against discourse, even as the amendment itself functions discursively and leads a distinctly discursive life.

If, as Foucault insists, freedom is a practice (rather than an achievement, condition, or institution), then the possibility of *practicing* freedom in the context of regulatory discourses occurs in the interstices of a given discourse as well as in resistance to the discourse.[11] In other words, the possibility can occur either within or against the discourse but is produced by the discourse in either case. Silence can function as speech in both kinds of practices of freedom, as becomes clear in the following anecdote offered by Foucault:

> Maybe another feature of [my] appreciation of silence is related to the obligation of speaking. I lived as a child in a petit bourgeois, provincial milieu in France and the obligation of speaking, of making conversation with visitors, was for me something both very strange and very boring. I often wondered why people had to speak.[12]

In a lecture at the Swedish Academy on the occasion of receiving the Nobel Prize for Literature, Toni Morrison also resets the conventional antinomy between silence and speech. Dwelling on the ambiguity of the power of language, she argues that certain kinds of language are themselves silencing, capable of violence and even murder, as well as themselves "susceptible to death, erasure":

> A dead language is not only one no longer spoken or written, it is unyielding language content to admire its own paralysis. Like statist language, censored and censoring. Ruthless in its policing duties, it has no desire or purpose other than to maintain the free range of its own narcotic narcissism, its own exclusivity and dominance. However moribund, it is not without effect, for it actively thwarts the intellect, stalls conscience, suppresses human potential. Unreceptive to interrogation, it cannot form or tolerate new ideas, shape other thoughts, tell another story, fill baffling silences. Official language smitheried to sanction ignorance and preserve privilege is a suit of armor, polished to shocking glitter, a husk from which the knight departed long ago.[13]

While Morrison is here concerned primarily with bureaucratic and other official languages, any language of regulation, including those originally designed on behalf of emancipation, has the potential to become official in the sense she describes. Indeed, language that cannot form or tolerate new ideas, language that cannot tell another story or fill baffling silences, language that functions as a suit of armor—such language would seem to characterize a number of progressive political discourses that have retreated from emancipatory aims and consolidated into institutional ones. Consider how both the discourses of liberalism and of Marxism came to function in this fashion, notwithstanding their original liberatory promise. Consider as well how often the language of political identity is today experienced as a policing language, even and especially by those whom the language intended to figure for emancipation. "A husk from which the knight departed long ago . . ."

Silence can be an effect of discourse; it can also function as resistance to regulatory discourse. And just as silenced discourses may contain elements of freedom, places unnoticed and hence unregulated by powerful interests, so their disinterring, even by the well-intentioned genealogist, can signal the end of their existence as a preserve for freedom. The latter is the subject of an extended meditation by Foucault about the problem of excavating subjugated knowledges:

> is it not perhaps the case that these fragments of genealogies are no sooner brought to light, that the particular elements of the knowledge that one seeks to disinter are no sooner accredited and put into circulation, than they run the risk of re-codification, recolonisation? In fact, those unitary discourses, which first disqualified and then ignored them when they made their appearance, are, it seems, quite ready now to annex them, to take them back within the fold of their own discourse and to invest them with everything this implies in terms of their effects of knowledge and power.[14]

Here, Foucault's concern is less with disrupting the conventional modernist equation of power with speech on one side and of oppression with silence on the other than with the ways in which potentially subversive discourse, born of exclusion and marginalization, can be colonized by that which produced it, much as countercultural fashion is routinely commodified by the corporate textile industry. While "disqualified" discourses are an effect of domination, they nevertheless potentially function as oppositional when they are deployed by those who inhabit them. However, when annexed by those unitary discourses to which they are in putative opposition, they become a particularly potent source of regulation, carrying as they do intimate and detailed knowledge of their subjects. Thus, Foucault's worry would appear to adhere not simply to the study but to the overt political mobilization of oppositional discourses. Consider, for example, how the discourse of multiculturalism has been annexed by mainstream institutions to generate new modalities of essentialized racial discourse; how "premenstrual syndrome" has been rendered a debilitating disease in medical and legal discourses; how "battered women's syndrome" has been deployed in the courtroom to defend women who strike back at their assailants by casting them as subrational, egoless victims of male violence; or how some women's response to some pornography was generalized by the Meese Commission on pornography as the violence done to all women by all pornography.[15]

Consider, more generally, attempts at codifying feminist discourses of women's experience in the unitary and universal discourse of the law. What happens when legal universalism's silence about women—that is, its failure to recognize or remedy the material of women's subordination—is remedied with discourses specifying women's experience and codifying the category of women through this specification? Catharine MacKinnon, for example, expressly aims to write "women's experience into law"; but as many other feminists have remarked, this begs the question of which women's experience(s), drawn from which historical moments, culture, race, and class strata, are to be recorded. Indeed, what does it mean to write historically and culturally circumscribed experience into an ahistorical discourse, the universalist discourse of law? Is it possible to do this without rendering "experience" as ontology and "perspective" as Truth, without unifying this ontology and this Truth in the Subject of Woman, and without encoding them in law as the basis of women's rights? What if, for example, the identity of women as keyed to sexual violation is an expressly late-twentieth-century and white middle-class construction of femininity, consequent to a radical deprivatization of sexuality on the one side and the erosion of other elements of compulsory heterosexuality—such as a severely gendered division of social labor—on the other? Moreover, does a definition of women *as* sexual subordinates, and the encoding of this definition in law, work to liberate women from sexual subordination, or does it, paradoxically, legally reinscribe femaleness as sexual violability? If the law *produces* the subjects it claims to protect or emancipate, how might installation of women's experience as "sexual violation" in the law reiterate rather than repeal this identity? And might this installation be particularly unemancipatory for women whose lived experience is not that of sexual subordination to men but that, for example, of sexual outlaw?

These questions suggest that in legally codifying a fragment of an insurrectionary discourse as a timeless truth, interpellating women as unified in their victimization, and casting the "free speech" of men as that which "silences" and thus subordinates women, MacKinnon not only opposes bourgeois liberty to substantive equality but potentially intensifies the regulation of gender and sexuality in the law, abetting rather than contesting the production of gender identity as sexual. In short, as a regulatory fiction of a particular identity is deployed to displace the hegemonic fiction of universal personhood, the discourse of rights converges insidiously with the discourse of disciplinarity to produce a spectacularly potent mode of juridical-regulatory domination.[16]

This problem is not specific to MacKinnon's work nor even to feminist legal reform, although it emerges with particular acuteness in both. Rather, MacKinnon's and kindred efforts at bringing subjugated discourses into the law merely constitute examples of what Foucault identified as the risk of recodification and recolonization of "disinterred knowledges" by those "unitary discourses, which first disqualified and then ignored them when they made their appearance." These efforts suggest how the work of breaking silence can metamorphose into new techniques of domination, how our truths can become our rulers rather than our emancipators, how our confessions become the norms by which we are regulated.

Though this kind of regulatory function is familiar enough to students of legal and bureaucratic discourse, it is less frequently recognized and perhaps more disquieting in putatively countercultural discourse, when confessing injury can become that which attaches us to the injury, paralyzes us within it, and prevents us from seeking or even desiring a status other than that of injured. In an age of social identification through attributes marked as culturally significant—gender, race, sexuality, and so forth—confessional discourse, with its truth-bearing status in a postepistemological universe, not only regulates the confessor in the name of freeing her, as Foucault described that logic, but extends beyond the confessing individual to constitute a regulatory truth about the identity group: confessed truths are assembled and deployed as "knowledge" about the group. This phenomenon would seem to undergird a range of recurring troubles in feminism, from the "real woman" rejoinder to poststructuralist deconstructions of her to totalizing descriptions of women's experience that are the inadvertent effects of various kinds of survivor stories. Thus, for example, the porn star who feels miserably exploited, violated, and humiliated in her work invariably monopolizes the feminist truth about sex work, as the girl with math anxieties constitutes the feminist truth about women and math; eating disorders have become the feminist truth about women and food, as sexual abuse and violation occupy the feminist knowledge terrain of women and sexuality. In other words, even as feminism aims to affirm diversity among women and women's experiences, confession as the site of production of truth, converging with feminist suspicion and de-authorization of truth from other sources, tends to reinstate a unified discourse in which the story of greatest suffering becomes the true story of woman. (This may constitute part of the rhetorical purchase of confessional discourse in a postfoundational epistemological era: confession substitutes for the largely discredited charge of false consciousness, on the one hand, and for generalized truth claims rooted in science, God, or nature on the other.) Thus, the adult who does not manifestly suffer from her or his childhood sexual experience, the lesbian who does not feel shame, the woman of color who does not primarily or "correctly" identify with her marking as such—these figures are excluded as bona fide members of the identity categories that also claim them. Their status within these discourses is that of being "in denial," of suffering from "false consciousness," or of being a "race traitor." This is the norm-making process in traditions of "breaking silence," which, ironically, silence and exclude the very persons these traditions mean to empower.

While these practices tacitly silence those who do not share the experiences of those whose suffering is most marked (or whom the discourse produces as suffering markedly), they also condemn those whose sufferings they record to a permanent identification with that suffering. Here, there is a *temporal* ensnaring in "the folds of our own discourses" insofar as our manner of identifying ourselves in speech condemns us to live in a present dominated by the past. But what if speech and silence aren't really opposites? Indeed, what if to speak incessantly of one's suffering is to silence the possibilities of overcoming it, of living beyond it, of identifying as something other than it? What if this incessant speech overwhelms not only the experiences of others but also alternative (unutterable, traumatized, fragmentary, or unassimilable) zones of one's *own* experience? Conversely, what if a certain modality of silence about one's suffering—and we might consider modalities of silence to be as varied as modalities of speech—*articulates* a variety of possibilities not otherwise available to the sufferer?

In *The Drowned and the Saved*, Primo Levi proffers drowning as a metaphor for the initial experience of entering a concentration camp, particularly for those who did not speak German or Polish: "filled with a dreadful sound and fury signifying nothing: a hubbub of people without names or faces drowned in a continuous, deafening background noise from which, however, the human word did not surface." This is a drowning in a world of unfamiliar as well as terrifying words and noise, a world of no civil structure yet so crowded with humanity that one's own humanness becomes a question. Primo Levi makes drowning function as a symbol for a lost linguistic order that itself signifies a lost civil order, for being at sea in words that do not communicate and by which one cannot communicate.[17] In a radically different context, Adrienne Rich also relates drowning to speech: "Your silence today is a pond where drowned things live."[18] Allowing, perhaps perversely, Rich's words to rest on Levi's, need her line only be read in its most obvious meaning—as an injunction to speak or die, a mandate to speak in order to recover the drowned things, recover life? What if the accent marks were placed differently, so that silence becomes a place where drowned things *live*—a place where Levi's drowning inmates survive despite being overwhelmed by the words that fill and consume the air necessary for life? What if the drowned things *live* in the pond, where it is silent, as they could not survive if brought back into the exposure of light and air, the cacophony of the camp? What if silence is a reprieve from drowning in words that do not communicate or confer recognition, that only bombard or drown?[19] Is this not one way also to understand the Constitution's Fifth Amendment, an amendment that was often seized as a literal lifeline by those the House Un-American Activities Committee persecuted in the 1950s?

This possibility, of course, is heavy with paradox insofar as drowning already signals death, and a pond where drowned things live therefore harbors death rather than life. But the paradox may be a productive one: perhaps there are dead or deadening (antilife) things that must be allowed residence in a pond of silence rather than surfaced into discourse if life is to be lived without being claimed by their weight. Certain experiences—concentration camp existence or childhood abuse—may claim their subjects and be conserved when they are incessantly remembered in speech, when survivors can only and always speak of what they almost did not survive and thus cannot break with that threat to live in a present not dominated by it. What if, too, this endless speaking about one's past of suffering is an attempt to expurgate guilt about what one did not do to prevent the suffering, an attempt that is doomed insofar as the speaking actually perpetuates the guilt by disavowing it?[20]

If to speak repeatedly of a trauma (which, by definition, carries wordless and even unintelligible content) is a mode of encoding it as identity, it may be the case that drowned things must be consigned to live in a pond of silence in order to make a world—a future—in parameters not fully given by the trauma. Put slightly differently by Primo Levi, "a memory evoked too often, and in the form of a story, tends to become fixed in a stereotype . . . crystallized, perfected, adorned, *installing itself in the place of the raw memory and growing at its expense.*"[21] Many contemporary narratives of suffering would seem to bear precisely this character; rather than working through the "raw memory" to a place of emancipation, discourses of survivorship become stories by which one lives, or refuses to live, in the present. There is a fine but critical distinction here between, on the one hand, reentering a trauma, speaking its unspeakable elements, and even politicizing it, in order to reconfigure the trauma and the traumatized subject, and, on the other hand, narrating the trauma in such a way as to preserve it by resisting the pain of it, thereby preserving the traumatized subject. While such a distinction is probably not always sustainable, it may be all that secures the possibility that we dwell in something other than the choice between a politics of pain and a politics of pain's disavowal.

To be sure, trauma is only one potential constituent of identity and its problematic relationship to speech and emancipation. Subordination is lived in many ways that have little or nothing to do with trauma. Thus, we might ask more generally if, by putting all into discourse, those attempting to emerge from a history of subordination do not risk sacrificing the rewards of any fragile hold acquired on autonomy and on the capacity to *craft* their lives and experiences rather than living almost fully at the behest of others. If, as Hannah Arendt maintained, some experiences "cannot withstand the glare of public light without being extinguished,"[22] do those traveling under the sign of queer, colored, or female not set at risk this recent, tenuous, and partial acquisition? Consider the pleasures of writing and other artistic practices, therapeutic work intended to fortify or emancipate rather than discipline (femininity) or "cure" (homosexuality), relatively uncoerced sexual lives, and some modicum of choice in reproductive and productive work. When all such experiences are put into discourse—when sexual, emotional, reproductive, and artistic lives are all exhaustively chronicled and thereby subjected to normativizing discourses—might this imperil the experiences of autonomy, creativity, privacy, and bodily integrity so long denied those whose subjugation included, *inter alia*, sexual violation or other deprivations of privacy? Are those subjected through sexuality, race, and gender so habituated to being without privacy and autonomy that they would compulsively evade and sabotage them? Do we presume we have nothing of value to protect from public circulation and scrutiny? Are we compelled to reiterate the experience of the historically subordinated: to be without a room of one's own, without a zone of privacy in which lives go unreported, without a domain of creativity free from surveillance—this time by our own eyes? Are we so accustomed to being watched that we cannot feel real, cannot feel our experiences to be real, unless we are watching and reporting them?

While there are disturbing ways in which the practice of compulsory discursivity would appear to recapitulate the historical, psychopolitical terms of subordinated subjects, there are also ways in which this practice coincides with a contemporary cultural tendency toward the glorification of banal personal experiences and unschooled opinions. Ours is a time of diarrhetic speech and publication—from the unfathomable amount of technical, political, commercial, and personal information that travels the Internet to the opinionated ignorance that animates much of A.M. talk radio. As many cultural critics have noted, notwithstanding or perhaps in proportion to the rise of illiteracy and aliteracy in the United States, today anyone's political opinion is worthy of the radio waves, and everyone's personal life is worthy of television exposure, a memoir, and, of course, a blog. Is this phenomenon, with its ability to displace world events and learned reflection, an effect of the confessional subject run amok, along with its hold on Truth in a post-foundational age? Or is it a kind of anxious filling of the void where meaning, profundity, and world history are said to have lived prior to their disenchantment? To what extent does the populist valorization of the common man, common sense, and the common experience recall the disdain for knowledge and reflection that was, historically, part of the material out of which European fascism was fashioned?

While each of these speculations may shed partial light on the explosion of banal and personal talk in the public media, the most important explanation may issue from a telling feature of this kind of expression—namely, that very little of it bears the character of either social connection or reflection. Most of this speech confesses, pronounces, or declares, and practically none of it is aimed at developing community with others or with working through experience or transforming understanding. In other words, speech that is aimed at bringing us together and that glorifies the common person paradoxically eschews the tonal and idiomatic material of connection. This paradox must be read as a symptom, and in particular a symptom of the predicament of the sovereign subject in a world of historically unparalleled global complexity and contingency. This subject who is so radically in need of external resources for understanding its context and production in our time is deprived of those very resources through pronunciative speaking. Indeed, the heavily defended creature conveys through this noncommuning speech, this tenacious dwelling in his or her own experience and opinion, a kind of rampant individual xenophobia that itself must be read as a terrible fear of disintegration or dissolution through connection, as the anxiety of an already profoundly weakened or disintegrated subject. The cult of personal experience and opinion, then, warns of the shakiness of the sovereign subject and of its extreme vulnerability to domination, even as this warning is expressed as a kind of hypersovereignty and hyperindividualism.

If the compulsion to put all into discourse can be read as a problematic remnant not only of particular histories of subordination but also of more generic anxieties of our time, then our capacity to be silent in certain venues might become the measure of our desire for freedom, including a desire to resist this discourse of anxiety masquerading as populism. The measure of this desire, of course, requires carefully distinguishing between the pleasures and freedoms of silence on the one hand and habituation to being silenced on the other. Also necessary is a second distinction between keeping one's counsel in order to articulate a spectrum of nonobvious possibilities and silence as the consummate gesture of passive aggression. Moreover, the desire for freedom requires not only the development of skills for silence but of skills for speech that is neither confessional nor normative in a moralizing sense (the latter, according to Nietzsche, is always a symptom of subordination or identification with subordination). Freedom requires the capacity for a kind of public speaking that neither demands concurrence from others nor entails the establishment of new norms by which to live; rather, this kind of speech willingly proffers ideas one would argue with and modify according to other characterologically public (as opposed to confessional) arguments.

It is tempting to end on this note. But it favors one side of a paradox about silence and silencing without recalling the other. For while silence can be a mode of resistance to power, including to our own productions of regulatory power, it is not yet freedom precisely insofar as it constitutes resistance to domination rather than its own discursive bid for hegemony. Put another way, one challenge to the convention of equating speaking with power and silence with powerlessness pertains to the practice of "refusing to speak" as a mode of resistance. Here, even as silence is a response to domination, it is not *enforced* from above but rather *deployed* from below: refusing to speak is a method of refusing colonization, of refusing complicity in injurious interpellations or in subjection through regulation.

Yet it would be a mistake to value this resistance too highly, for it is, like most rights claims, a defense in the context of domination, a strategy for negotiating domination, rather than a sign of emancipation from it. In *The Alchemy of Race and Rights*, the black legal scholar Patricia Williams coins a provocative phrase that captures this feature of silence as discourse. Following a disturbing encounter with some obnoxious young students who jostled her off the sidewalk in a largely white college town, she speaks of "pursuing her way, *manumitted into silence*."[23] In this paradoxical locution, Williams intimates that purchased emancipation from slavery conferred a right to silence, one to which, however, she is also condemned. "Manumitted into silence"— emancipated into silence—no longer a subject of coerced speech, no longer invaded in every domain of her being, yet also not heard, seen, recognized, wanted as a speaking being in the public or social realm. Perhaps then, one historical-political place of silence for collective subjects emerging into history is this crossed one: a place of potentially pleasurable reprieve in newly acquired zones of freedom and privacy, yet a place of "freedom from" that is not yet freedom to make the world.

SIX

■ ■ ■ ■

FEMINISM UNBOUND: REVOLUTION, MOURNING, POLITICS

WE ARE convened in Belfast to ask what women's studies is, what feminism might be, "beyond sex and gender."[1] This beyond is a strange place, if it is indeed a place, where it is proposed that the subject and object of the field might be left behind even as the field persists. It is a place where the "what" and the "we" of feminist scholarly work is so undecided or so disseminated that it can no longer bound such work, where the identity that bore women's studies into being has dissolved yet oddly has not dissolved the field itself. Or is it not a place but a time, this beyond of sex and gender? Are we proposing to be *after* sex and gender, no longer bound by them or perhaps no longer believing in them, and yet, in the peculiar offering that only temporality makes, bringing along what we are after even as we locate it behind us?

If feminist scholarship came into being through the analytic circumscription of sex and gender, being feminist scholars beyond or after sex and gender is not the same as dispensing with them but rather, perhaps, is more like being after the Fall, after their fall. Fallen yes, but like all toppled sovereigns and overthrown founders they do not thereby cease to govern. ("The dead are mighty rulers," Freud reminds us, prophesying among other things his own continued hovering over our work.) So we are compelled, now that we know the impossibility of circumscribing gender without participating in its construction and regulation, and now that we know the indissociability of sex and gender from race, caste, class, nation, and culture, to think feminism and women's studies in this condition of afterness, in this temporal condition of "knowing better" about our naive yet founding past, and thus also to grieve what we now know we never should have loved . . . a tortured and guilty grieving to be sure. What is the cost of such grieving, not just to ourselves, but to this field that lives on after the death of its subject and object? And if we are not grieving, if we are only delighted to be "beyond sex and gender," what then is the quality of this afterness, what parasitic relationship to a past that it does not love do these practices maintain?

But wait! A place and a time beyond sex and gender—wasn't this also the revolutionary feminist dream? Wasn't feminism born of the utopian aspiration to make a world in which sex and gender would become history as significant markers of human difference, as vehicles of inequality and injury, as keys to life possibility, as ways of distinguishing worth, potential, humanity from its other? How and when did sex and gender become essential objects of feminism rather than that which we aimed to overthrow? No, the question has to be put differently now: what kind of feminism aims to conserve rather than reduce, eliminate, or at the very least diffuse sex and gender? If women's studies has difficulty imagining itself beyond sex and gender, this would seem to confess its contemporary investment in their persistent social, political, psychic, or economic importance, thus locating a non-revolutionary sensibility and aim at the core of women's studies. Women's studies invested thus comes after the loss of revolutionary feminism; it figures itself as a non-utopian enterprise with more than a minor attachment to the unhappy present.

In this light, I want to turn the question of the future of women's studies a bit, to ask not whether feminism and feminist scholarship can live without sex or gender, but how it lives, and will continue to live, without a revolutionary horizon. Not how we may thrive in the aftermath of the dissemination of our analytical objects, but *what are we* in the wake of a dream in which those objects were consigned to history? What does it means for feminist scholars to be working in a time after revolution, after the loss of belief in the possibility and the viability of a radical overthrow of existing social relations? What kind of lost object is this? Revolution belongs to modernity and whatever our respective orientations toward the value of modern versus postmodern *thought*, there is little question that *the time* of modernity is no longer securely ours, that key elements of modernity are waning, that if we are not "beyond" modernity we are most certainly "post" modernity. The post, of course, is a complex transitional and conjunctural moment, one in which we continue to live "with" what we are also "after." This living with is uneasy work: ghosts and ungrieved losses clutter a present and future that are anything but sure-footed. "We suffer," Marx reminds us, "not only from the living, but from the dead. [Indeed], *le mort saisit le vif!*"[2]

MOURNING REVOLUTION

What do we mourn when we imagine we are mourning revolution today? Something has died but we argue over what the body is (there will turn out not to be a body). A unified Left? Reason? Social totality? Marxism? Belief in the Good, the True, and the Beautiful? Hope? Grand narratives? Utopia? The promise of the twentieth century? Love of the world? Modernity? Humanity? Is radical transformation itself no longer imaginable, or is it the fantasy of human control over human destiny that has vanished? Or are we stymied at conjuring postcapitalist, postpatriarchal, postcolonial social, economic, and political forms that could emancipate and satisfy all and each? Is it a postrevolutionary vision that eludes us today?

Since grief inevitably recalls prior and contiguous losses, perhaps settling on a single object is not so important: whatever we are mourning most immediately might be the scene for discovering all that has gone unmourned for a feminist Left in our time. But such discovery is not easily won: the condition of mourning is a stumbling and stuttering one, a condition of disturbed ground, of inarticulateness, of disorientation in and about time. A mourning being must learn to walk again, on ground once secured by the now lost object, a process that makes palpable how contingent firm and level ground always is. Indeed, in mourning, one discovers horizons, banisters, firmaments, and foundations of life so taken for granted that they were mostly unknown until they were shaken. A mourning being also learns a new temporality, one in which past meets future without moving through a present (in which the present all but vanishes) yet also one in which the future is unmoored from parts of the past, thus puncturing conceits of linearity with a different way of living time. In mourning, too, the solidity of the subject falters: even as one may be "consumed by grief" and so retreat from the world, grief also diminishes the subject undergoing it, undermining illusions of autonomy and self-constitution, revealing hitherto unknown dependencies and the limits of agency, mocking the will's desire to project itself backward and forward in time.

Revolution, the world turned upside down, through which modernity entered history, which modernity would perfect and by which modernity would be perfected, appears today both anachronistic and unprecedentedly dangerous. Anachronistic because political, economic, and social powers are dispersed, and thus the reins of society cannot be grasped, perhaps do not even exist. Unprecedentedly dangerous because the technologies available to counterrevolutionary forces, and to states in particular, are deadly beyond compare—these include not only the weapons of physical warfare but technologies of organization, infiltration, intelligence, interrogation. Dangerous too because all visions of the Good now appear to consort with fundamentalism. (It is telling that the only time revolution was meaningfully invoked in the last quarter century was to describe the transformation of Iran following the rise of Ayatollah Khomeini.) If regimes of truth are inevitably totalitarian, what remains of emancipatory claims about the best way to order and govern human beings? How even to endeavor to transform the present, whatever totalitarian elements it might harbor, without tapping this danger? Perversely, this sensitivity to fundamentalism would seem to consign us to the present, not because it is freer or in other ways better than the alternatives, but because the pursuit of concrete alternatives inevitably implicates us in the deliberate imposition of a truth, as opposed to negotiating or passively living under one. The post-Enlightenment feminist Left is politically neutered, and neutralized, by this formula: If there is always a governing political truth, at least let *us* not be the fundamentalists; if every regime is an Occupation, at least let us not be the occupying force. Thus have we lost the capacity to imagine ourselves in power, self-consigned instead to the rancorous margins in which we are at best a permanent heckle to power.

For Hannah Arendt, modernity yields the radically new modality of political change, revolution, from the convergence of three principles constitutive of the age: (1) the rise of "the social question," which above all denaturalized mass poverty as inherent in the human condition; (2) the centering of *freedom* as a human need or right; and (3) a historical consciousness that embraced the possibility of *novelty* and the conviction that the course of history could suddenly begin anew. It is when "the idea of freedom and the experience of a new beginning . . . coincide,"

Arendt argues, that revolution in the modern sense is possible and takes the specific form of the rise of the oppressed to displace their oppressors and the regime that privileged them.[3] There is another singular feature of modernity that makes revolution its spirit, namely the progressivism that suffused modern philosophies, histories, and political dreams, the historiography that operated at the level of moral and political conviction that human existence on all fronts—freedom, prosperity, equality, civility—was steadily improving. It is via this progressivism that the other meaning of revolution, a naturalistic phenomenon that cannot be stopped—as in the earth revolving around the sun—conjoins with the agentic features of popular uprising for bread or freedom to capture the inevitability of such uprisings and even the inevitability of their eventual triumph.[4] In the age of freedom, equality, and new beginnings, revolution emerges as the term for a continuous and inexorable push for the realization of these values against the old regimes that denied them both legitimacy and actuality. Left revolutionaries of the twentieth century placed themselves in this tradition—the press of the poor and the outcast for a freedom and equality that was their unquestionable modern entitlement, the unstoppable force of democratization, the realization of "true human emancipation," indeed, the realization of modernity's promise around the globe.[5]

It is this conviction about the inevitable triumph of the people over the illegitimate powers of wealth and rule that exploit, dominate, or disenfranchise them whose loss washes over us today. What has been drained from the present is not only faith in the capacity of revolution to dethrone corrupt or illegitimate power but the standing of this capacity as a beacon of the spirit of the age. Gone is the belief in radically breaking with history; equally eviscerated is the notion of inexorable progress toward freedom and the related notion that an innate human desire for freedom is one—if not the—engine of history. Shattered too is the conviction that the future belongs to the downtrodden, that power is ever anything but illegitimate, that equality, freedom, and well-being for the many are inevitable, let alone possible.

The promise of revolution delivered by the Enlightenment was premised upon presumptions about the emancipatory nature of reason and the capacity of human beings to make their own history. It was a promise that, unfettered by tradition and legal subjection, reason would carry its human subjects to truth, freedom, and equality. This is also the conceit of social contract theory from Hobbes to Rousseau to Rawls: under the reign of reason, human beings could consciously and deliberately fashion their world, vanquishing gods, kings, and other superhuman forces as makers of history and polities. Reason, knowledge, truth, and freedom against power—this was the formula that poststructuralist insight discredited in relocating power to the inside of those ostensibly emancipatory forces. But even before this insight took hold, twentieth-century events had largely devastated the Enlightenment promise: the two world wars; the Shoah; the Naqba; the merciless pillaging of the Third World by the First; socialist revolution turned brittle, brutal, then gray; decolonization turned to bloody authoritarianism and corruption; the calculated geopolitical instrumentalization of the Third World by cold war powers; the materialization of a form of global capitalism unprecedented in its reach and capacities for deracinating human lives; and a final decade featuring a rise in violent ethnonationalisms literally unimaginable to Kantian universalists half a century earlier.

As the promise of the twentieth century darkened, its shadow lengthened over the already foundering hopes of the Enlightenment and modernity—hopes for a steady improvement of the human condition, hopes rooted in the progress of liberty and the inevitable spread of equality, hopes tethered to the revolutionary spirit but in its calmer register.[6] A promise and hopes that seem to have died before their time, except Gillian Rose recalls that for something to have died prematurely involves imagining a time when death would be nothing, possible only when life is nothing, when death comes to what already does not matter.[7] This very nothingness, Rose argues, was already contained within modernity (Weber reads Tolstoy as revealing how progressivism, especially in knowledge, empties life of meaning and knowledge of its truth value) and is deepened, according to Rose, by "postmodern" formulations in which history is not charted by progress, inherent purpose, a drive toward an end, or toward anything.[8] Yet if modernity was always only a promise, then fruition is not its telos; rather, modernity's achievement *was* this promise. When the promise dies, it does not take our earthly goods and activities but our sense of futurity, and the future is the place where almost all meaning is harbored for the modern progressivist consciousness. The nihilism so often attributed to "the postmodern" is not a draining of meaning from the present—where meaning can thrive even and sometimes especially in the wake of God and Truth—but a draining of the future from present meaning, a loss of redemption in Benjamin's sense. Mourning revolution is thus mourning a particular kind of futurity, a specifically modernist kind of rightful expectation, a temporality we do not yet know how to live without.

In mourning revolution, we are not mourning dead bodies, but rather the insufficiently dead body of the past, the failure to have sacrificed enough of the present for a different future, the failure to have killed off substantial parts of the past, to have really broken with them as only revolution can and thus to have cast them into the past. In mourning the insufficiency of deaths, we mourn the promise that collective human will can come between past and future, that a humane future will rise out of a vanquished inhuman past. We mourn the promise that history can be taken in hand, that mind can have its way with the world, that we are destined to nothing except to be free of determination by history.

The death of a promise is like no other because a promise is incorporeal; there is no body to claim, to bid farewell, to bury (which is why the Left argues incessantly over what the body is). In mourning a dead promise, a promise that no longer is one, we mourn "the disappeared"; this is a perpetual and ungratified mourning that reaches in vain for closure. The very object that we mourn—the opening of a different future, the ideal illuminating that future—has vanished. So we cannot even see or say what we mourn, gather at the site of its disappearance, weep over its remains, hold its lively embodiment in our memory as we must if the mourning is to come to an end. This is a mourning that inevitably becomes melancholia—as the loved and lost promise becomes nameless and unfathomable in a present that cancels and even mocks it, its disappearance is secured by this loss of a name and so also is our inconsolability. Melancholia too because if we experience the promise as not simply dead but betrayed, we are divided against our love for it—love betrayed but not given up is love that literally does not know where to house itself.

SOCIALIST AND FEMINIST REVOLUTIONS

The contemporary Euro-Atlantic Left is in mourning not just for the idea of revolution as a political modality, but for two particular revolutionary dreams that died in the last quarter of the twentieth century. One, very roughly, could be called socialist. The other, equally roughly, could be called feminist and sexual. Intertwined in complex and differing ways for different segments of the New Left, both carried the utopian promise by which our worldview as well as our orientation toward critical theory was framed. It is not easy to disentangle the collapse of a revolutionary modality at a generic level from the collapse of these particular projects of transformation; our mourning is confusing and confused here. Are we grieving a particular radical vision or radical vision as such? Or is it revolutionary cultural-political life that we are at once embarrassed by and pining for?

The New Left attachment to socialist revolution—which was never merely about economic justice, rather, its promised fruit included a panoply of betterments in human and nature-human relations—is difficult to loosen, notwithstanding the concrete failures of state socialism. Without replacing a profit-driven economic system by one rooted in common ownership and ordered by thoughtfulness about the complex needs of humans and their habitat, it is difficult to conceive not simply the relief of economic desperation on the part of the many but building and sustaining social forms that could cultivate modest generosity, security, equality, peaceability, mental and physical health, and responsible relations with nature. But that replacement is remote to the point of vanishing today.

What happened to the dream of socialist revolution is tediously familiar. State socialism is economically unviable in a capitalist world order—inefficient, uncompetitive, impoverished. Nor does it emancipate: work is no less alienating, no more under the control of the worker, no more organized for immediate human needs, no more engaging of human creativity, no less dreary, than under any other regime. But if not state socialism, which was never the revolutionary dream anyway, then what? World socialism? Organized by what scandalously centralized global powers? Self-governing interdependent villages? In what version of history? The loss here, then, is not just a revolutionary agent or impulse, nor is it just the odds for revolutionary success. The problem is that it is nearly impossible to conceive of an emancipatory, ecological, and economically capacious socialism that could follow upon the current development of what Marx referred to as "productive forces," that is compatible with contemporary political, economic, or social organizations of space and populations, and that is incorruptible by what we now know to be the many and dangerous ways of power.

Feminist revolution—which was never merely about sexual equality but, rather, carried the promise of remaking gender and sexuality that itself entailed a radical reconfiguration of kinship, sexuality, desire, psyche, and the relation of private to public—went awry somewhat differently. Given the loss of the socialist possibility, there were limits to its realizability; but reckoning with limits is not the same as reckoning with absolute loss, and the feminist ambition to eliminate gender as a site of subordination could technically be met within a capitalist life form—that is, there is nothing in sexed bodies or even in gender subordination that capitalism cannot live without. The stakes in the old arguments about whether feminist revolution required a socialist one were largely contoured by a male Left dubious about whether feminism was ultimately radical or bourgeois, whether gender subordination was a primary or derivative contradiction in the social order, whether it was truly material in the present or mainly attitudinal, the "muck of ages" not yet washed away. This configuring diverted attention from the most crucial connection between New Left and revolutionary feminist aims. It is clear enough that women and men can be rendered interchangeable cogs in a contemporary and future capitalist machinery, where physical strength is rarely at issue, where continuity on the job matters little, where reproductive work has been almost completely commodified and reproduction itself is nearly separable from sexed bodies and is in any event separable from a sexual division of labor. Notwithstanding the protracted Marxist-feminist analyses of the indispensability of unpaid housework to the production of surplus value, the home as a necessary if stricken haven in a heartless world, and the need for a malleable surplus army of labor (all of which were straining to prove both the materiality of gender subordination and its necessity to capitalism), it is evident enough today that the equal participation and remuneration of women in the economic and civic order can be achieved, if unevenly and with difficulty.

Capitalism neither loves nor hates social differences. Rather, it exploits them in the short run and erodes them in the long run. In Marx's poetics, capitalism "batters down Chinese Walls," leveling and homogenizing every aspect of culturally and traditional differentiation that it subjects to "its naked cash nexus."[9] Capitalism commodifies and reifies sexual difference even as it steadily erodes the ground of this difference in biology, the sexual division of labor, and the productive and reproductive functions of the family. Capitalism does not require gender subordination or even gender any more than it requires racial subordination or race; it has tendencies that augment as well as tendencies that attenuate such subordination; social movements and public policies can abet one or another tendency or both simultaneously. So the critical question for feminist revolution does not concern the inherent relationship of capitalism to gender subordination at the level of political economy. Rather, the critical question is whether what potentially issues from subordination, namely a radical critique of systemic injustices and suffering and a radical vision of alternatives, can be sustained in a capitalist social order over time and take shape as viable and organized opposition. What fuels or depletes a lived consciousness of the inhumanity, irrationality, or simply unsatisfying nature of current arrangements and the impulse to make a different order of things? What sustains a willingness to risk becoming different kinds of beings, a desire to alter the architecture of the social world from the perspective of being disenfranchised in it, a conviction that the goods of the current order are worth less than the making of a different one? It is this capacity to develop and sustain a critique and a vision of the alternatives that contemporary capitalism undermines so effectively with its monopoly on the Real *and* the imaginable, with the penetration of its values into every crevice of social and subjective existence, and with its capacity to discursively erase if not concretely eliminate alternative perspectives and practices. Without another conscious vantage point from which to perceive, criticize, and counter present arrangements, a vantage point Herbert Marcuse argued largely vanished in postwar capitalism, it is almost impossible to sustain a radical vision as realistic or as livable.[10] And it is almost impossible to fight for something not on the liberal and capitalist agenda, a fight largely incompatible with seeking freedom *from* that agenda.

In the Euro-Atlantic world, there was one decade in the last half century in which this other dimension was carved out in the form of political subcultures. The political upheavals and formations of the Sixties included the production of a cultural-political and epistemological outside that allowed utopian visions to stake more than utopian claims, to be sustained by and partially lived out in the subcultures themselves. In Eastern Europe, this decade came later and had a different political valence, one fueled by the ambition to topple state communism and one whose utopian vision was limned by the imagined (and overdrawn) freedom of "the West."[11] In both cases, though, what was so heady about these cultural-political formations, what made their risks and deprivations utterly worthwhile to the participants, was not merely the anticipation of a beautiful new world to come nor merely the effect of a popular political potency rarely felt in late modernity—it is not clear that either Sixties radicals in the West or Eighties dissidents and intellectuals in the East felt such potency much of the time. Rather, in both cases, a radical protest of the status quo was lived out in a highly charged subculture that was as libidinally compelling as a group experience can be, a revolutionary erotics that paradoxically bound its participants precisely by inciting challenges to all conventional bonds—those containing intellectual work within the academy, those restricting love and sex to the family, and, above all, those separating eros, politics, ideas, and everyday existence from one another. When poetry becomes political, when politics becomes erotic, when thinking is de-commodified and comes to feel as essential to life as food and shelter, not only do ordinary fields of activity become libidinally charged, but this desublimated condition itself betokens (however illusorily) an emancipated world to come. This revolutionary awakening of the mind and the senses carries (however falsely) a promise of living beyond repression, alienation, compartmentalization, indeed beyond settled forms or institutions *tout court*. It is difficult to avoid nostalgia for the irreverent and transgressive spirit coursing through these brief, out-of-history times when all social practices—from marriage to literature to architecture—are open to rethinking and refashioning. Boundary-smashing Eros saturates the social form . . . which is also why it cannot last.

However problematically, this formation of political life and possibility carried at its heart attachment to both political and individual transformation, a deep conviction about the possibility of making humans differently, and pleasure in the powers both of critique and of collective action. Revolutionary feminism promised that we could become new women and men, that we could literally take in hand the conditions that produce gender and then produce it differently, that not simply laws and other institutions could be purged of gender bias but that humans themselves could be produced beyond gender as history has known it. Nor was this revolutionary feminist impulse circumscribed only by feminism's second wave and its convergence with the New Left. Rather, it can be traced from Wollstonecraft to feminists of the French and Russian Revolution to novelists, poets, and theorists of the revolutionary moment of the second wave in North America and Europe. This was feminism that imagined humanity one day free of gender as a social production, just as the ideal of communism figured humanity not simply emancipated from class but free of domination by necessity. Androgyny was one version of this feminist vision, but there were other formulations that worked with the possibility of difference delinked from subordination.

As philosophically and politically naive as this belief appears in retrospect, we are still compelled to ask: What is feminism without it, without the conviction that the deep conditions of gender subordination—and not only the laws that encode it or the norms that regulate it—can be identified and transformed? What suspicion about the naturalness of gender subordination persists when feminism addresses only the wrongs done to women but not *the socially produced capacity for women to be wronged*, to be victims? What inevitable entanglement with a politics of *ressentiment* tinges feminism if the problem is always one of how women are *treated by* power, if the fix always entails taming power (obtaining protection through law or regulation), if we cannot figure a world in which we imagine governing ourselves *and* imagine release from the identity that has been the site of our injury? Feminism without revolution means giving up on seizing the conditions through which gender is made, and it is the illusion of such a seizure—the illusion that the conditions are distinct, objectifiable, and could be taken in hand—that we have necessarily abandoned. If we learned from de Beauvoir that women are made not born, it was first Marxist, then psychoanalytic, and then Foucauldian feminism that illuminated not only how extensive and elaborate but finally how beyond human grasp this making is, the degree to which it is bound up not just with attitude, law, and custom, not just with a sexual division of labor, not just with racial, caste, and class stratifications, not even just with the psychic economies of families and their deposits in gendered subjectivities, but also with myriad social norms buried in discursively organized practices ranging from motherhood to microchip assembly to the military. If revolution was undermined by the collapse of Enlightenment formulations of social totality, reason, truth, freedom, progress, and history, it was also undone by a confrontation with the subterranean byways and nesting places of power, and with power's intangible, dispersed, unconsolidated, and non-unified operations. Yet feminism without revolution, conjoined with theories of intricate social construction, comes close to producing a critique of male dominance with almost no exit. Only fools call this situation the "triumph of biology," though clearly the fools have the monopoly on the press these days.[12]

But what precisely killed the revolutionary *spirit* of second wave feminism? This question is inseparable, of course, from what dispersed or destroyed the more general radical spirit of that epoch, a story too complex to rehearse here. There are specifics for feminism, though, worth considering. First, even as revolutionary feminism itself gave birth to lesbian separatism and various feminist nationalisms bound to race and ethnicity, in crucial ways these offspring had a more conservative *Weltanschauung* than their progenitors—tending toward the consolidation rather than the disruption of identity, often inward turning in their politics, less consistently critical of capitalism and liberalism, more inclined toward interest-bound reformism than with propounding a comprehensive vision for society. It goes without saying that these movements importantly expanded the operative substantive definitions of woman and feminism. To identify politically conservative tendencies in these movements does not vitiate this achievement; rather it refuses to index the radicalism of a political program according to this achievement. Certainly it is possible to expand the subject of feminism while narrowing feminism's political vision.

Second, within the academy, there were serious consequences of the contingent historical fact that sexuality studies emerged as revolutionary feminism waned. For all of its intellectual and political fecundity, sexuality studies often hit a slightly reactionary note on the question of transforming male-dominant regimes of gender. This was not simply ignorance or misogyny on the part of an initially male-dominated academic industry, although these were present and took their toll, but rather a consequence of the erotics carried in existing gender arrangements. Here, Catharine MacKinnon must be credited with grasping something important and deadly about sexual life in male-dominant regimes: the eroticization of gender subordination constitutes the major (not the only) erotic economy of such regimes. So, when the focus is on the politics of sexuality rather than the politics of sexism, that which aims to eliminate gender subordination by undermining the grounds and performance of gender difference can appear at the same time to be opposing sexual pleasure. Thus does revolutionary feminism come to be figured as antisexual, and thus does a certain reification of gender difference (regardless of how it is distributed across biologically sexed bodies) appear as a means of reappropriating the erotics that feminism would otherwise seem to degrade or aim to eliminate.

Third, feminism emerging from the Third World and the former Soviet bloc was routinely represented in the West as uninterested in or even hostile to critiques of femininity or compulsory heterosexuality, and consequently as uninterested in critiques of the family, marriage, gendered subjectivity, etc. When combined with many Third World feminists' suspicion of male "revolutionaries" and the overt hostility of many Chinese, Russian, and East European feminists to Marxist regimes and to the infelicitous communist state regulation of gender and the family, feminism in the Second and Third Worlds came to be figured as an indictment of a decadent and indulgent radicalism of First World feminism.

Taken together, these three sources of rejection of revolutionary Euro-Atlantic feminism tarred it as self-indulgent, white, unconnected to the real needs of most of the world's women, and/or as opposed to pleasure and antisexual. But the forces disintegrating revolutionary feminism did not only come from without. Within Western feminist theory, poststructuralist insights were the final blow to the project of transforming, emancipating, or eliminating gender in a *revolutionary* mode. This may seem counterintuitive when such insight is often considered responsible for theorizing gender as a resignifiable and at least modestly flexible fiction, and makes such rich use of the Nietzschean-Foucauldian understanding that regimes of domination inadvertently produce subversive subjects and forms of agency opposed to such regimes. The point is not that poststructuralism undermines the project of transforming gender but that it illuminates the impossibility of seizing the conditions making gender as well as the impossibility of escaping gender. Indeed, in its very challenge to the line drawn in the revolutionary paradigm between "conditions" and "effects," it undermined the possibility of objectifying those conditions and of conceiving agents who could stand outside them to transform them. Moreover, poststructuralist feminism's appreciation of the psychic coordinates and repetitions constitutive of gender locates much of its production in social norms and deep processes of identifications and repudiations only intermittently knowable to its subjects, even less often graspable, and thus unsuited to a paradigm of transformation premised upon seizing and eliminating the conditions producing and reproducing gender. Certain gender conventions or norms might be resisted, subverted, or resignified but resistance and resignification are not equivalent to a transformation of *the conditions* of gendered erotics, conditions that are no longer posited as outside of its subjects, and hence are not ours to mastermind but at best only to resist or negotiate.

Thus, gender is regarded (and lived) by contemporary young scholars and activists raised on poststructuralism as something that can be bent, proliferated, troubled, resignified, morphed, theatricalized, parodied, deployed, resisted, imitated, regulated . . . but not emancipated. Gender is very nearly infinitely plastic and divisible, but as a domain of subjection with no outside, it cannot be liberated in the classical sense, and the powers constituting and regulating it cannot be seized and inverted or abolished. In one crucial respect, then, gendered regimes can be seen to share a predicament with global capitalism: each is available to almost any innovation and possibility except freedom, equality, and collective human control. Each is beyond the reach of revolution.

BEYOND REVOLUTION

Historically outmoded, exhausted as an ambition, ruptured as political ontology, discredited by contemporary political epistemology—revolution is unquestionably finished. Why, though, would we mourn it? Quite simply, this death seems to carry with it our dreams for a better world. Notwithstanding much brave left talk about "localism," "coalition politics," "postidentity politics," and "resistance," without revolution, it is hard to see how our political labors—intellectual or otherwise—enable the radical transformation of the current order into a more just, free, and egalitarian one. Our critique of the present is not matched by prospects for transformation—there are neither credible alternatives nor credible roads to them. A severe critique that does not articulate with anticipation of a different future . . . an illness with no cure . . . how to proceed when this has become our condition? What, under these circumstances, are the alternatives to despair, melancholy, or resignation?

Most common today is the impulse to retrench the critique to fit the apparent horizon of possibility. "Don't criticize what you cannot change" or "Don't dwell on the problem if you don't have a solution" are the unspoken maxims of the age. Accordingly, a substantive critique of capitalism (and not just its putatively recent "globalized" form), critiques of marriage and the family, critiques of mass-mediated culture, indeed critique itself have all largely fallen off a left intellectual and political agenda. But such retrenchment only compounds left despair insofar as reconciliation to the contours and content of the present abandons the unique political orientation of the Left itself, one that calls into question existing social arrangements to argue for more just and humane ones. So, what possibilities are there for living and working, without bitterness or disavowal, in this difficult theoretical and political place, this place of critique that exceeds realizability, of indicting more than we can repair or replace? What as yet unpracticed political sensibility is required to dwell here?

A second widespread inclination is to blame our stymied condition on "Them" (the neocons, the Right, the Feminist Backlashers, various political or corporate Masters of the Universe) or on some loathed part of "Us" (sectarian identity politics, poststructuralism). This move forecloses attention to what has brought us to this pass and also limits discernment of troubling political formulations and formations born from it, e.g., rejection of critique, state-centered reformism that veers into intensified regulation, or left feminist politics reduced to relatively impotent protest and complaint. Moreover, the impulse to blame and complain tends to displace any impulse to develop strategies for the assumption of power; it necessarily entrenches rather than repairs from the condition it bemoans. Its very crankiness is a recognizable symptom of mourning.

If the modality of political transformation in modernity was revolution, what lies beyond it? What is the "beyond" of this loss and how does the loss itself open the field of this beyond? What are the possible postrevolutionary modalities of radical political and social transformation in our time? Revolution was always finest in its opening of possibility, in the sensibility and practices of political risk, imagination, upheaval, questioning, and vision this opening incited. By contrast, the lowest point in revolution was usually its furious will to power distilled into fundamentalism—Bolshevik authoritarianism, the Cultural Revolution, Napoleon and/or the Terror, in its own way even the Constitutional Convention of the United States. The nonpolitical "revolutions"—scientific, industrial, informational—also inverted their emancipatory impulse as they achieved hegemony or took institutional root; as regimes each contains critique, delimits what is thinkable, sayable, and doable, erects its truth as deities. Every revolution's Thermidor arrives with ferocious certainty about what should follow the openings produced by upheaval, about how the promise will be realized, about the indifference of the means to the end; this surety precisely reverses the spirit of upturning and opening toward an uncertain future that makes revolutionary intellectual and political agitation so heady and fecund, so full of imagination and possibility. How, then, to cultivate the fecundity of revolutionary opening without the revolutionary push toward the knowable and the controllable? How to cultivate this remainder of revolution in the form of a utopian imaginary stripped of its promise to redeem the past and be realized in the future? Above all, how to suspend this utopian impulse in a different temporality such that it could fuel rather than haunt or taunt left political life in our time? Our task would seem to be that of prying apart an exuberant critical utopian impulse from immediate institutional and historical solutions so that the impulse can survive stumbling, disorientation, disappointment, and even failure and so that the impulse remains incitational of thought and possibility rather than turning fundamentalist. The task, then, would be to recuperate a utopian imaginary absent a revolutionary mechanism for its realization such that this imaginary could have a political use, that is, participate in the making of social transformation and not only constitute an escape from the felt impossibility of such transformation. Such a recuperation locates a radical politics apart from left fundamentalism on the one side, and apart from the refusal to reckon with deep social and economic powers entailed in liberal political pluralism on the other. This is the political ground between postrevolutionary despair or paralysis and resignation to liberal reformism itself no longer convincing in its narrative of incrementalism. A radical democratic critique and utopian imaginary that has no certainty about its prospects or even about the means and vehicles of its realization, that does not know what its imagined personae will be capable of—this would seem to be the left political sensibility that could give our mourning a productive postrevolutionary form.

Feminism and Women's Studies
beyond Sex and Gender

Women's studies "beyond sex and gender" does not seem to me a right naming of our problem. Rather, the very perception of it as a problem is a symptom of a condition in which women's studies has not simply lost its revolutionary impulse but has turned against this impulse, against its desire to have done with these objects. It is a symptom of a condition in which feminism's investment in its own career advancement has replaced the political impulse to overthrow itself, to lose its boundaries both by becoming part of a larger order of transformative politics and by being washed away in such politics. So what if we folded women's studies "beyond sex and gender" into recuperating the project of emancipating sex and gender, thereby breathing a renewed emancipatory spirit into women's studies? This requires shaking off nostalgia for the big bang theory of social change, a nostalgia that generates either hopelessness or conservatism, often amounting to the same thing in the form of resignation. But, perhaps even more importantly, this requires a certain dwelling in that state of mourning in which a seemingly unendurable loss is also the opening of possibility to live and think differently. For this, we have to understand not only what has been lost, but also who we now are as thinking, political beings who both were formed by and lost a certain critical promise. In mourning a dead promise, we also have the gift of being able to parse the promise, distinguishing what we want to carry with us as a life force from what, at best, is hard knowledge or painful de-idealization.

On the one hand, only by stumbling, only by feeling what one depended on before and with what one can now replace that dependency, does a mourning being begin to discern possibility in loss, in being free of an object that seemed like life itself. If we are without revolutionary possibility today, we are also free of revolution as the paradigm of transformation: what new political formations might be born from this moment? On the other hand, avowing our loss allows us to cultivate the memory—and with Benjamin, ignite that memory—of the utopian imaginary of the revolutionary paradigm and so make that imaginary part of our knowledge for working in the present, not just a lament about the unrevolutionary present. What if feminism "beyond sex and gender" could become a site for recuperating utopian aims without the mechanism of revolution? What if it could become the site for developing postrevolutionary modalities of political thought and practice? What if we let our objects fly?

SEVEN

■ ■ ■ ■

THE IMPOSSIBILITY
OF WOMEN'S STUDIES

THERE is today enough retrospective analysis and harangue concerning the field of women's studies to raise the question of whether dusk on its epoch has arrived, even if nothing approaching Minerva's wisdom has yet emerged. Consider the public arguments about its value and direction over the past half decade: Is it rigorous? Scholarly? Quasi-religious? Doctrinaire? Is it anti-intellectual and too political? Overly theoretical and insufficiently political? Does it mass-produce victims instead of heroines, losers instead of winners? Or does it turn out jargon-speaking metaphysicians who have lost all concern with Real Women? Has it become unmoored from its founding principles? Was it captured by the radical fringe? The theoretical elite? The moon worshippers? The man-haters? The sex police? Perhaps even more interesting than the public debates are the questions many feminist scholars are asking privately: Why are so few younger scholars drawn to women's studies? Why are many senior feminist scholars, once movers and shakers in the making of women's studies programs, no longer involved with them? How did women's studies lose its cachet? Is it a casualty of rapidly changing trends and hot spots in academe, or has it outlived its time or its value in some more profound sense? Does it continue to secure a crucial political space in male-dominated academia? What is the relationship between its political and its intellectual mission?

I want to consider a problem to one side of these questions that might also shed light on them. To what extent is women's studies still tenable as an institutionalized domain of academic study, as a circumscribed intellectual endeavor appropriate as a basis for undergraduate or graduate degrees? Given the very achievements of feminist knowledge about foundations, identities, and boundaries over the last two decades, what are the intellectual premises of women's studies now? What are the boundaries that define it and differentiate it from other kinds of inquiry? These are not abstract questions, but ones that issue from the very real conundrums currently faced by those of us in women's studies. Consider the following examples from my own program, one that is formally strong and robust with its five full-time faculty, two hundred majors, and introductory courses that annually enroll more than seven hundred students (and hence reach nearly one-quarter of the undergraduate population of the university as a whole).

In the early nineties, Women's Studies at the University of California, Santa Cruz, undertook that frightening project of self-scrutiny known as curriculum revision. What brought us to this point is itself interesting. For a number of years, we had maintained a set of requirements for the undergraduate degree that comprised an odd mix of the academically generic and the political, requirements that were not coined all at once as a coherent vision of a women's studies curriculum but rather had been pieced together in response to various and conflicting demands as the program developed. *The generic*: students were required to take a three-term sequence consisting of "Introduction to Feminism," "Feminist Theory," and "Methodological Perspectives in Feminism," a sequence marked by category distinctions notably at odds with the expansive understanding of theory, the critique of methodism, and the challenge to a meaningful divide between the humanities and social sciences that are all putatively fundamental to feminist inquiry. This meant that quite often our first project in these courses was to undo the very distinctions we had given ourselves, thus repeating our founding rebellion against disciplinary distinctions, this time in our own house. *The political*: the only other content-specific requirement for the major was a course called "Women of Color in the United States," in which students gained some exposure to the histories, literatures, and cultures of Asian American, African American, Latina, and Native American women, and white students in the course learned to "decenter themselves" while women of color spoke.

This strange combination of genres in the curricular requirements schooled our students in the isolated intellectual (and putatively non-racialized) character of something called theory, the isolated (and putatively nontheoretical) political mandate of race, and the illusion that there was something called method (applied theory?) that unified all feminist research and thinking. Most of the students loved the experiential and issue-oriented introductory course, feared theory, disliked methods, and participated somewhat anxiously in the "Women of Color" class. Hence, most women's studies students regarded the requirements as something to be borne, and the major as having its rewards in the particulars of the elective courses they chose, or in the feminist community of students the major harbored. Moreover, the limited and incoherent nature of these requirements as a course of study meant that our students were obtaining their degrees on the basis of rather impoverished educations, something women have had too much of for too long.

But what happened when we finally sat down to revise the curriculum is even more interesting than the desires symptomatized by the existing curriculum—in particular, the desire for disciplinary status signified by the claim to a distinct theory and method (even as women's studies necessarily challenges disciplinarity), and the desire to conquer the racialized challenge to women's studies' early objects of study by institutionalizing that challenge in the curriculum. In our curriculum revision meetings, we found ourselves completely stumped over the question of what a women's studies curriculum should contain. Since, in addition to trying to produce a curriculum that would express the range, depth, and problems occupying women's studies scholarship, we were also trying to address faculty frustration about students not being well enough trained in anything to provide rewarding classroom exchange in the faculty's areas of expertise, we focused intently on the question of what would constitute an intellectually rigorous as well as a coherent program. We speculatively explored a number of different possibilities—a thematically organized curriculum, pathways that roughly followed the disciplines, more extensive requirements in each domain of feminist scholarship that the faculty considered important—but each possibility collapsed under close analysis. Each approach seemed terribly arbitrary, each featured some dimension of feminist scholarship that had no reason to be privileged, each continued to beg the question of what a well-educated student in women's studies ought to know and with what tools she ought to craft her thinking. We also found ourselves repeatedly mired by a strange chasm between faculty and students in the program: A majority of our majors were interested in some variant of feminist sociological or psychological analysis—experientially, empirically, and practically oriented— or in studies of popular culture. Yet not one of our core faculty worked in sociology, psychology, community studies, communications, or film/video. Many of our students wanted to think, learn, and talk about body image and eating disorders, gender and sexuality in the media, sexual practices, intimate relationships, sexual violence, how children and adolescents are gendered, and survivor identities ranging from alcohol to incest. Our five core and three most closely affiliated faculty are trained respectively in American literature, American history, Chinese history, English literature, Renaissance Italian and French literature, Western political theory, European history, and molecular biology. As feminist scholars, clearly we have strayed from the most traditional boundaries of these fields, just as we have learned and taught material relatively unrelated to them, but even this reformation of our training and scholarly orientation could not close the gap between the students' interests and our own.

If the practical project we set for ourselves in revising the curriculum was running aground, certainly we were in the grip of an important historical-political problem. Why, when we looked closely at this project for which we had fought so hard and which was now academically institutionalized, could we find no there there? That is, why was the question of what constituted the fundamentals of knowledge in women's studies so elusive to us?[1] We were up against more than the oft-discussed divide between "women's studies" and feminist theory, the political insidiousness of the institutional division between "ethnic studies" and "women's studies," a similarly disturbing division between queer and feminist theory, or the way that the ostensibly less identitarian rubric of "cultural studies" promised but failed to relieve these troubling distinctions. And we were up against more than the paradox that the disciplines which have been so radically denatured in recent years are also apparently that which we cannot completely do without, if only to position ourselves against them within them. We were also up against more than the dramatic fracturing of women's studies as a domain of inquiry during the last decade—the fact that contemporary feminist scholarship is not a single conversation but is instead engaged with respective domains of knowledge, or bodies of theory, that are themselves infrequently engaged with each other. And we were up against more than the ways that this decade's theoretical challenges to the stability of the category of gender, and political challenges to a discourse of gender apart from race, class, and other markers of social identity, constituted very nearly overwhelming challenges to women's studies as a coherent endeavor. We were up against more than the fact that many of the intellectual impulses originally forma-tive of women's studies have now dispersed themselves—appropriately, productively, yet in ways that profoundly challenged the turf that women's studies historically claimed as its own, especially the terrain of sexuality and of race.

We were up against more than any one of these challenges because we were up against all of them. And together, they called into question the quarter-century-old project of institutionalizing as curriculum, method, field, major, or bachelor of arts what was a profoundly impor-tant political moment in the academy, the moment at which women's movements challenged the ubiquitous misogyny, masculinism, and sexism in academic research, curricula, canons, and pedagogies. Indis-putably, women's studies as a critique of such practices was politically important and intellectually creative. Women's studies as contempo-rary institution, however, may be politically and theoretically incoher-ent, as well as tacitly conservative—incoherent because by definition it circumscribes uncircumscribable "women" as an object of study, and conservative because it must resist all objections to such circumscrip-tion if it is to sustain that object of study as its raison d'être. Hence the persistent theory wars, race wars, and sex wars notoriously ravaging women's studies in the 1980s, not to mention the ways in which women's studies has sometimes greeted uncomfortably (and even with hostility) the rise of feminist literary studies and theory outside of its purview, critical race theory, postcolonial theory, queer theory, and cultural studies. Theory that destabilizes the category of women, racial formations that disrupt the unity or primacy of the category, and sexu-alities that similarly blur the solidarity of the category—each of these must be resisted, restricted, or worse, colonized, to preserve the realm.[2] Each, therefore, is compelled to go elsewhere, while women's studies consolidates itself in the remains, impoverished by the lack of challenges from within, bewildered by its new ghettoization in the academy, this time by feminists themselves.

If uncertainty about what constitutes a women's studies education is a persistent whisper in all undergraduate program development, it positively howls as a problem at the level of graduate training. Since our program has regularly been invited by our administration over the past decade to submit a plan for a graduate program, we have strug-gled repeatedly to conjure the intellectual basis for a Ph.D. program in women's studies. In what should the graduate student in women's studies be trained? What bodies of knowledge must a women's studies doctoral candidate have mastered and why? Which women should she know about and what should she know about them? Which techniques of analyzing gender should she command and why? Ethnography or oral history? Lacanian psychoanalysis? Quantitative sociological analysis? Object relations theory? Literary theory? Postcolonial criticism? Neo-Marxist theories of labor and political economy? Social history? Critical science studies? There is a further question: Who are we to teach these things simply because we are interested in feminism and feminist analyses from our own scholarly perspectives?

The unanswered question of what women's studies is also manifests itself in day-to-day concerns about what may count as a women's studies course and who may count as an affiliated member of a women's studies faculty. Almost all women's studies programs rely on faculty and curricular offerings in other departments, both because they are too small to do otherwise and because of the proud interdisciplinarity undergirding the intellectual project of women's studies. But if political devotion to the cause (once the main criterion for who is in women's studies and who is not) no longer serves as the measure for what constitutes a women's studies course, what does? Must such a class be focused solely or primarily on women? (What of feminist courses on other topics, such as feminist science studies or studies in masculinity, and what of nonfeminist courses concerned with women?) Must the class be taught from a feminist perspective? (What counts as such a perspective and who decides?) Is it a class that potentially contributes to feminist theory and research? (Don't most well-conceived courses in the social sciences and humanities potentially make such a contribution?)

For many women's studies programs, the difficulty of deciding these things leads to some strange curricular formations: Chaucer taught by one faculty member may count for women's studies, but not when it is taught by another; "Introduction to Sociology" does not count but a course called "The Chicano Experience" does; philosophy courses on phenomenology are excluded but courses on Saussure and Derrida are included; "Early Modern Europe," taught by a feminist historian, counts, but "Modern Europe," taught by a nonfeminist, does not; similarly, Lacan taught by a lesbian feminist semiotician counts while Lacan taught by an avant-garde art historian and filmmaker does not; an anthropology course called "Queer Political Cultures" counts but one called "Peoples and Cultures of the American Southwest" does not. And then there is the endless petitioning. A student wants to know if her invertebrate biology course, in which she focused intensely on biological discourses of mating, might count—and why not? Another student wonders whether he can include his history of political theory courses—and what better background for grasping the antecedents of feminist political theory? A student complains that her "Psychology of Women" course, listed as a women's studies elective, mostly trafficked in unreconstructed psychological behaviorism and was not feminist at all. Another petitions to have her passion for psychoanalytic feminism certified as legitimate by letting her count all her studies in Freud and Klein as part of her feminist education. Especially given the strange routes by which most faculty arrived in women's studies, and given the diverse materials we draw upon to vitalize our own research, who are we to police the intellectual boundaries of this endeavor? And how did we become cops anyway?

. . . .

Certainly when peered at closely, the definitions of all disciplines wobble, their identities mutate, their rules and regulations appear as contingent and contestable. Most disciplines, founded through necessary exclusions and illusions about the stability and boundedness of their objects, have reached crises in their attempts to secure their boundaries, define an exclusive terrain of inquiry, and fix their object of study. And in most cases, the desire to persist over time has resulted in a certain conservatism or its close cousin, methodism. Thus for sociology to sustain the radicalism that was one strain of its founding, rather than becoming nominalist and positivist, it had to connect with political economy, politics, semiotics, and history, as a small branch of it did. Similarly, the contemporary battles in literary studies can be understood, in part, as turning on the question of whether literature's object of study shall remain fixed and narrow, or shall become much more indeterminate and broad in scope, up to and past the point where the objects constituting the identity of the discipline—literary texts—are regarded as contingent and even dispensable.

There is something about women's studies, though, and perhaps about any field organized by social identity rather than by genre of inquiry, that is especially vulnerable to losing its raison d'être when the coherence or boundedness of its object of study is challenged. Thus, paradoxically, sustaining gender as a critical, self-reflexive category rather than a normative or nominal one, and sustaining women's studies as an intellectually and institutionally radical site rather than a regulatory one—in short, refusing to allow gender and women's studies to be disciplined—are concerns and refusals at odds with affirming women's studies *as* a coherent field of study. This paradox will become clearer as I turn to what I take to be one of the central problematics of feminist inquiry today, and one of the central conundrums facing women's studies: how to come to terms with the problem of the powers involved in the construction of subjects.

This problem is also shaped by a paradox. On the one hand, various marked subjects are created through very different *kinds* of powers— not just different powers. That is, subjects of gender, class, nationality, race, sexuality, and so forth are created through different histories, different mechanisms and sites of power, different discursive formations, different regulatory schemes. On the other hand, we are not fabricated as subjects in discrete units by these various powers: they do not operate on and through us independently, or linearly, or cumulatively. Insofar as subject construction does not take place along discrete lines of nationality, race, sexuality, gender, caste, class, and so forth, these powers of subject formation are not separable in the subject itself. These powers neither constitute links in a chain nor overlapping spheres of oppression; they are not "intersectional" in their formation (Kimberle Crenshaw), they are not simply degrees of privilege (Aida Hurtado), and they cannot be reduced to being "inside or outside, or more or less proximate to, dominant power formations" (Patricia Hill Collins).[3] As so many feminist, postcolonial, queer, and critical race theorists have noted in recent years, it is impossible to extract the race from gender, or the gender from sexuality, or the masculinity from colonialism. Moreover, to treat various modalities of subject formation as additive in any of the ways suggested by the terms above is to elide the way subjects are brought into being through subjectifying discourses. We are not simply oppressed but *produced* through these discourses, a production that is historically complex, contingent, and occurs through formations that do not honor analytically distinct identity categories.[4]

For feminist theory, the most problematic dimension of this paradox pertains to the fact that grasping subject construction for different forms of social subjection (class, race, etc.) requires distinctive models of power, yet subject construction itself does not unfold according to any one of these models because we are always more than one, even if we participate in the norms of some and the deviations of others. Not simply the content but the modalities of power producing gender, race, or caste are specific to each production—the mode of production and dimensions of state power that produce class, and the discourses and institutions of normative heterosexuality that produce gender, are largely noncomparable forms and styles of power. Thus, for example, understanding the way in which class and gender are regulated by various discourses of class and gender is not a matter of applying a neutral "apparatus" of regulation to the specific problem of class and gender. There is not, as Judith Butler recently remarked, first gender and then the apparatus that regulates it; gender does not exist prior to its regulation.[5] Rather, the gendered subject emerges through a regulatory scheme of gender—we are literally brought into being as gendered subjects through gender regulation. From this perspective, the very idea of a regulatory "apparatus" appears as a kind of structuralist Althusserian hangover clouding the Foucauldian insight into the radical reach of subject production through regulatory discourse. In Foucault's understanding of the power that circulates through the subject of regulation, there can be no actual apparatus because there is no sharp distinction between what is produced and what is regulating— we are not simply targets but vehicles of power.[6] Thus, to paraphrase Nietzsche awkwardly, we must be able to conceive regulation without the regulator, to understand regulation as only and always materializing in its effects, and to understand these effects as specific to that which is being regulated.

This problem can be put the other way around: the forms of power that produce gender or produce class are themselves saturated with that production—they do not precede it. Indeed, it is this element of subject production that makes intelligible the very notions of masculinist power, or bourgeois power, as opposed to speaking about gender and class power simply in terms of rule by one group of people and the oppression of another. In the more conventional way of speaking about power as an instrument of domination interchangeable among groups and even individuals, power is cast as a (gender-, class-, and race-) neutral means of achieving privilege and domination. Power is conceived as something held by particular individuals or groups, and this commodity status gives it independence from the bearer of it and the subject of power. It is this (mis)conception of power that allows various forms of oppression to be spoken of in additive and interchangeable terms. Power, in this pre-Foucauldian view, is seen to locate subjects in a field of power, but the field is not itself seen to produce the subjects it locates; it is not regarded as the very medium of emergence of those subjects.

Law is one quite fertile place to see the effects of the conundrum that distinctive models of power are required for grasping various kinds of subject production, yet subject construction itself does not transpire in accordance with any of these models. I want to ponder this domain at some length, in order to shed light from outside the field of women's studies on the problem of the subject that it faces. Through a consideration of the ways that different kinds of marked subjects appear in law and legal studies, we can reflect on the difficulties that women's studies encounters in its simultaneous effort to center gender analytically and to presume gender's imbrication with other forms of social power.

Bracketing the sphere of formal and relatively abstract antidiscrimination law, where discrimination on the basis of a laundry list of identity attributes and personal beliefs is prohibited, it is unusual to find the injuries of racism, sexism, homophobia, and poverty harbored in the same corners of the law. These injuries are rarely recognized or regulated through the same legal categories, or redressed through the same legal strategies. Consequently legal theorists concerned with these respective identity categories are not only engaged with different dimensions of the law depending on the identity category with which they are concerned—for example, feminists might focus intently upon family law while working-class activists might be more closely engaged with contract and labor law. In addition, they often figure the law itself in quite incommensurate ways. Consider, as an example of the latter, the debate about the value of rights between critical legal theorists, concerned about the function of property rights in producing the very existence of workers, tenants, the poor, and the homeless, and critical race theorists, concerned with enfranchising historically rights-deprived members of subordinated racial groups. While critical legal theorists tend to regard rights as entrenching and masking inequality, many critical race theorists have figured rights as vital symbols of personhood and citizenship, as the very currency of civic belonging in liberal constitutional orders. More interesting than brokering this debate in terms of the relative validity of the arguments is recognizing what each argument makes visible that the other does not. The neo-Marxist perspective of the critical legal theorists emphasizes the convergence of formal legal equality with the tendency of other liberal and capitalist discourses to naturalize class inequality and the social powers constitutive of class, including those powers conferred by legal rights. The histories of slavery and the civil rights movement out of which arises the critical race theory position, in contrast, emphasize the extent to which rights discourse historically has designated who does and does not count as a member of human society: if rights signal personhood, then being without them is not merely to be without a concrete asset, but to lack the less tangible but equally essential degree of civic belonging they confer.

Both claims are important and compelling, but can both be true? Can the same juridical discourse obscure and articulate social inequality, serve as an instrument of entrenching inequality and as a means of redressing it? This question appears less paradoxical when it is recognized that what the critical legal theory position makes visible are certain mechanisms of socioeconomic inequality in liberal and capitalist societies, while the critical race theory claim about the symbolic value of rights highlights discursive strategies of marginalization and dehumanization.[7] These are two different forms of power and subjection, sometimes converging in a common subject and injury, sometimes not. While both are relevant to class as well as race, the former probably has a heavier bearing for class and the latter for race. Because the powers formative of class and of race are so different, it should not surprise us to discover that they bear different relationships to crucial legal categories. What is difficult, of course, is determining how to navigate these differences when one is dealing with race and class subordination in a single subject. Indeed, it is in the place where race and class converge (in a poor, racially stigmatized population) that the operation of rights becomes deeply paradoxical. This problem becomes even more complex when one considers the category of gender, where both socioeconomic deprivation and dehumanization operate as part of what constitutes women as such: clearly women need the "rights of man" in order to establish their place in humanity, yet, as countless feminist theorists have also pointed out, these same rights will not only fail to address but will mask many of the substantive ways in which women's subordination operates.[8]

Consider other examples of the ways the law itself is figured differently by those invested in different social categories and social identities. The sodomy statutes that quite literally constitute the homosexual legal subject, and constitute it as an always already criminal subject, have no obvious parallel in the making of race, gender, or class.[9] There are no similarly taboo practices that both identify and criminalize the racialized, gendered, or class subject. Nor is there, in the production and regulation of these other subjects, an analogy to the prohibition on same-sex marriage or the lack of a secure legal status for homosexual parenting. On the other hand, the equality/difference dilemma faced by feminist legal reformers has no parallel in theorizing about race or class and rarely surfaces in discussions of gay rights. There would appear to be no equivalent, in the operation of homosexual, racial, or class subjection, to the conundrum of maternity, or even of sexual and physical violability and vulnerability, in defining the central problematic, and central paradoxes, of feminist legal reform. More generally, there is no equivalent to the crucial place of reproductive rights for women's equality in defining the parameters of racial freedom, or ending the stigma for minority sexual orientation.[10] Within liberal legalism, no distinctive domain of control equivalent to that of women over reproduction stands as a *condition* of freedom and equality for homosexual and racially marked subjects. Beyond liberal legalism it was Marx, of course, who argued that collectivization of the means of production was exactly such a condition for the working class, but even this possible parallel breaks down when the importance of collective ownership and control for workers is contrasted with women's need for individual control over their reproductive bodies.

The heated debate among advocates of lesbian and gay legal reform about whether gayness is immutable (genetically rooted) also has no parallel in other domains of identity-based critical legal theory. While there is certainly much discussion about gender's mutability among feminist theorists and activists, and much controversy about hypothesized racial differences, these discussions have not entered the legal fray in the same way as the "gay gene" debate, nor could one imagine them occupying the place that the mutability debate has in queer theory and legal reform. The central question in the legal version of the immutability debate is not simply about whether sexual preference is genetically coded and hence determined prior to the emergence of desire. Rather, the debate revolves around whether it best serves homosexuals to represent themselves as unable to be other than what they are, and hence as discriminated against if they are subjected to unequal treatment, or, conversely, whether it is strategically wiser to concede not only the mutability but even the temporal contingency and ambiguity of sexual preferences and practices, and to root antidiscrimination claims in a program of sexual freedoms relevant to all sexualities. It is hard to imagine a parallel to this debate in other domains of legal politics, such as those concerned with race or gender, since it has never become part of popular consideration to imagine that we have a choice in these identities, or that the markers of those identities are radically contingent or ambiguous.

Given such differences in the formation and legal inscription of different marked subjects, it is unsurprising that concern with securing certain legal terrain does not simply vary, but often works at cross purposes for differently marked identities. Earlier I offered the example of conflicts over the general value of rights. Privacy functions in a similar way. For many feminists, the legal and political concept of privacy is a highly ambivalent one insofar as, historically, "the private" has functioned to depoliticize many of the constituent activities and injuries of women—reproduction and caring for children, domestic violence, incest, unremunerated household labor, emotional and sexual service to men. Yet for those concerned with sexual freedom, with welfare rights for the poor, and with the rights to bodily integrity historically denied to racially subjugated peoples, privacy appears as an unambiguous good. Indeed, the absence of a universal right to privacy constitutes the ground on which Hardwick's bedroom was invaded in*Bowers v. Hardwick*. This absence was also the legal basis for decades of surprise visits by social workers to enforce the "man in the house rule" for welfare recipients. Like rights themselves, depending upon the function of privacy in the powers that make and position the subject, and depending upon the particular dimension of marked identity that is at issue, privacy will sometimes be regarded as advancing emancipatory aims, sometimes deterring them; in some cases it will be seen to cloak the operation of inequality, while in others it will be seen as assisting in the elaboration of equality doctrine.

Nor is it only categories, problems, and domains of law that vary across different modalities of social subjection. Approaches to law vary as well, depending upon the modality in question, since law is understood to carry and deploy these different powers in disparate ways. Thus racism, understood by most critical race theorists as omnipresent in legal argument yet less frequently explicit in legislation and adjudication, has necessitated the development of a critical practice for excavating the racism in legal textual narrative. Much critical race theory involves close readings of the narrative strategies and devices—including symbol, metaphor, metonymy, and analogy—upon which judicial opinion draws when discussing race or racialized cases. This is an analytic practice, however, that neither feminist jurisprudence, nor

critical legal theory concerned with class, nor most queer legal theory
has followed: each has been more inclined to expand or rework the
formal legal categories that overtly carry the power of gender, class,
and homosexuality.[11]

I have chosen critical approaches to the law as a way of highlighting
diversity in the production and regulation of different marked subjects
because law's formal purpose in liberal constitutional orders is to redress the injuries occasioned by unjust distributions of power, and the
purpose of critical theoretical engagements with legal doctrine has
been to more closely specify such power. Consequent to this attention
to power, the ensemble of critical practices aimed at reforming juridical practices of justice vis-à-vis particular identities highlights something often mentioned but rarely followed for its implications in
feminist theory: formations of socially marked subjects occur in radically different modalities, which themselves contain different histories
and technologies, touch different surfaces and depths, form different
bodies and psyches. This is why it is so difficult for politically progressive legal reformers to work on more than one kind of marked identity
at once. This is why it is nearly impossible to theorize a legal subject
that is not monolithic, totalized by one identity category, and cast as
identical with other subjects in that category. We appear not only in
the law but in courts and public policy either as (undifferentiated)
women, or as economically deprived, or as lesbians, or as racially stigmatized, but never as the complex, compound, internally diverse and
divided subjects that we are. While this could be seen as a symptom of
the law's deficiency, a sign of its ontological clumsiness and epistemological primitivism, more significant for purposes of this essay is what
it suggests about the difficulty of analytically grasping the powers
constitutive of subjection, a difficulty symptomatized by the law's
inability either to express our complexity or to redress the injuries
carried by this complexity.

In other words, the problem of representing and redressing the construction, the positioning, and the injuries of complex subjects is not
just the law's problem with power, but ours. It is a problem that can
only be compounded by programs of study that feature one dimension
of power—gender, sexuality, race, or class—as primary and structuring. And there is simply no escaping that this is what women's studies
does, no matter how strenuously it seeks to compensate for it. Indeed,
the notoriously fraught relationship of women's studies to race and
racism can be understood as *configured* by this dynamic of compensation

for a structural effect that can never be made to recede, even as it is frantically countered and covered over. Insofar as the superordination of white women within women's studies is secured by the primacy and purity of the category gender, *guilt* emerges as the persistent social relation of women's studies to race, a guilt that can be undone by no amount of courses, readings, and new hires focused on women of color. Indeed, consider again the curriculum I described early in this essay in which "women of color in the United States" is the one group of women our students are *required* to learn about. Consider again that most students' experience of this course is primarily emotional— guilty, proud, righteous, anxious, vengeful, marginalized, angry, or abject. And consider, too, that alumnae of that course often relay these feelings, highly mediated, into other women's studies courses as criticisms of the syllabi, the student constituency, or the pedagogy in terms of a failure to center women of color, race, or racism. Faculty, curriculum, and students in women's studies programs are in a relentless, compensatory cycle of guilt and blame about race, a cycle structured by women's studies original, nominalist, and conceptual subordination of race (and all other forms of social stratification) to gender.

• • • •

To reiterate, the paradoxical moment in the problem I have been discussing comes with the recognition that despite the diverse and often even unrelated formations of the subject according to race, class, nation, gender, and so forth, subject construction itself does not occur in discrete units as race, class, nation, and so forth. So the model of power developed to apprehend the making of a particular subject/ion will never accurately describe or trace the lines of a living subject. Nor can this paradox be resolved through greater levels of specificity in the models themselves, for example, mapping the precise formation of the contemporary "middle-class Tejana lesbian." This subject, too, is a fiction insofar as there are always significant elements of subjectivity and subjection that exceed the accounting offered by such lists. There will always be those who feel misdescribed by such descriptions even as they officially "fit" them. Perhaps even more importantly, this kind of excessive specificity sacrifices the imaginative reach of theory, inevitably moving toward positivism, and in this way repeats the very eclipse of sociohistorical powers it was intended to challenge: these powers become fixed as categories of analysis, rendered as adjectives and nouns, rather than historicized and theorized. Finally, this kind of specificity in identity description and analysis tacitly reiterates an understanding of power as only domination: the powers named in these supposedly complex appellations or "subject positions" always refer to vectors of social stratification that figure social power in terms of hierarchy. That is, "white middle class" is presumed to convey two lines of privilege while "Third World woman" is presumed to convey two lines of subjugation. Power is seen not as producing the subject, but only as privileging or oppressing it.

To conclude this excursus into the question of subject production, as feminism has for many become irreversibly connected to the project of multicultural, postcolonial, and queer analysis, terms such as "multiplicity," "intersections," "crossroads," "borderlands," "hybridity," and "fracturing" have emerged to acknowledge—without fully explaining or theorizing—the complex workings of power that converge at the site of identity. The currency of these terms suggest the limitations of existing theories of both power and history for articulating the making of subjects, and especially gendered subjects. For this work of articulation, I would argue that we need a combination of, on the one hand, analyses of subject-producing power accounted through careful histories, psychoanalysis, political economy, and cultural, political, and legal discourse analysis, and, on the other, genealogies of particular modalities of subjection that presume neither coherence in the formations of particular kinds of subjects nor equivalence between different formations. In other words, what is needed is the practice of a historiography quite different from that expressed by notions of cause and effect, accumulation, origin, or various intersecting lines of development, a historiography that emphasizes instead contingent developments, formations that may be at odds with or convergent with each other, and trajectories of power that vary in weight for different kinds of subjects. The work I am describing involves serious and difficult research, arduous thought, and complex theoretical formulations—it will not be conducive to easy polemics or slogans in battle. And it will add up neither to a unified and coherent notion of gender nor to a firm foundation for women's studies. But it might allow us to take those powerful founding and sustaining impulses of women's studies—to challenge the seamless histories, theories, literatures, and sciences featuring and reproducing a Humanism starring only Man—and harness them for another generation or two of productive, insurrectionary work. However much it is shaped by feminism, this work will no longer have gender at its core and is in that sense no longer women's studies. To the extent that women's studies programs could allow themselves to be transformed—in name, content, and scope—by these and allied projects, they will be renewed as sites of critical inquiry and political energy. To the extent that they refuse this task, and adhere to a founding and exclusive preoccupation with women and feminism, they will further entrench themselves as conservative barriers to the critical theory and research called for by the very scholarship they incited and pedagogical practices they mobilized over the past two decades.

. . . .

Some final thoughts and rejoinders. Among those committed to women's studies who are cognizant of the problems and incoherence of the field, the usual arguments on behalf of sustaining and building women's studies programs are mounted in expressly political language. Women's studies, it is said, remains the primary site for feminist consciousness-raising among students, and for feminist agitation in university life as a whole. Moreover, given the historical struggle to institutionalize women's studies programs through the establishment of departments or the procurement of full-time faculty positions, the idea of radically transforming their direction such that they are no longer identified primarily with women or even gender seems as if it could only signal that the opposition was right all along. In other words, most of us assume that there remains irrefutable political value to women's studies programs and intractable political constraints against friendly challenges to women's studies programs, and that this value and these constraints must override whatever is troubling about women's studies' intellectual aporias.

I share this assumption to a degree, but the problem with allowing it to serve as the justification for maintaining women's studies programs as they are is that it renders dispensable a deep and serious intellectual basis for women's studies, just as it disregards the erosion of that basis as something less than a challenge to women's studies' raison d'être. Indeed, by privileging the political over the intellectual, the intellectually strategic over the intellectually sound, and by effectively conceding that these operate on separate planes, these arguments affirm the status of women's studies as something distinct from the rest of the university's intellectual mission for research and teaching. In effect, by admitting its thoroughly politicized rationale, these defenses replicate the low value that hostile outsiders often accuse women's studies of attaching to the caliber of arguments and to intellectual life as a whole; suspicions about the non- or anti-intellectual dimensions of women's studies are thus confirmed. Equally problematic, these arguments affirm this nonintellectual mission for something wholly and uniquely identified with women, and what could be more detrimental to feminist aims? How, indeed, could such an understanding of women's studies constitute it as a credible basis from which to influence university curricula and life?

I am not arguing that the struggle to establish women's studies programs was misbegotten nor am I suggesting that women's studies is entirely void of rich intellectual content. Rather, I am making a specific historical argument. There is an unimpeachable importance to the last two decades of developing scholarship, of feminist teaching across the university, and of feminist influences on administrations, incited by the struggles centered on developing women's studies programs. Without doubt we are everywhere now, and without doubt this "we" was literally brought into being by the fight to establish and legitimate women's studies. But the strategies and ambitions that produced this effect at one historical moment are not necessarily those that will sustain or enhance it at another. Feminist scholars must ask whether the very institutional strategies that once fomented rich and exciting intellectual endeavor now work against it, or work against the currents that might be its most fruitful future.

There is another question to be raised here. If the mission of women's studies is understood as primarily political, and as willingly sacrificing intellectual coherence and aims to its political project, who will teach in such programs and what kind of teaching will it be? Without discounting the varied degrees and types of political aims that many of us bring to our academic work, it is one thing to craft and mobilize these aims in the course of one's teaching and research and quite another to function within an intensely politicized space in which intellectual life and standards are often regarded as secondary concerns. Many contemporary feminist scholars currently have limited traffic with women's studies programs—they may cross-list a course or two, or allow their names to be affiliated with the program, but remain peripheral to the curriculum and governance of the program. Conversely, many women's studies programs are staffed by a disproportional number of faculty with an attenuated relationship to academic research and writing, but whose political devotion to feminism, and emotional devotion to the students, is often quite intense. More and more, feminist scholarship is spun from sites other than women's studies programs. And more and more, women's studies faculty are not using this scholarship; sometimes they are explicitly hostile to it.

Rather than assigning blame for this complex and painful dynamic, let us note instead some of its effects. First, the anti-intellectualism discussed above is increasingly codified as the spirit of women's studies work, while the gap widens between the ethos and curriculum of women's studies and the rest of the humanities, arts, and social sciences. Second, while women's studies once served to legitimate and support, in a positive way, feminist scholarship across the academy, it would now seem to legitimate it negatively by allowing feminist scholars in other disciplines to tacitly define themselves and their work *against* women's studies. Women's studies has come to be perversely useful to some academic feminists as "the other" against which respectable feminist scholarship is defined.

Is it possible to radically reconfigure women's studies programs without sacrificing the feminism they promulgate among students and help keep alive at universities? We might ask this question another way, by asking whether teaching feminist courses, including basic courses such as "Introduction to Feminisms" "Introduction to Feminist Theories," and "Histories and Varieties of Women's Movements" must be done in the context of a degree-granting program or whether the discussions we had long ago about "mainstreaming" (moving these courses into the general curriculum of other disciplinary and especially interdisciplinary programmatic sites) might be revived. To retain such course work without containing it within women's studies might allow us to reconfigure women's studies programs without such a move appearing as a neoconservative victory in favor of a return to "traditional curricula." And it might allow us, too, to insist that students of feminism and feminist theory learn the appropriate antecedents and cognates to these topics, for example, the emergence of the struggle for women's emancipation in the context of democratic and socialist revolutions in the West, or the relevance of Rousseau, Marx, Freud, and more recent philosophical and literary thinkers to feminist thought and practice. In this regard, consider how difficult it is to teach contemporary feminist theory to students who share none of the intellectual referents of the feminist theorists they are reading. What a difference it would make to develop those background knowledges as part of students' work in philosophy, cultural studies, literature, anthropology, or critical theory so that students were actually armed to engage and contest the arguments they encounter in feminist theory and in postcolonial, queer, and critical race theories as well.

Still, am I, in the end, suggesting that we never should have developed and institutionalized women's studies programs? Absolutely not. Without doubt, women's studies constituted one of the most vibrant and exciting contributions to the American academy in the 1970s and 1980s. Moreover, I believe there are large and complex lessons to be developed—about institutionalizing identitarian political struggles, about conflating the political with the academic, and about late modern forms of disciplinarity—from the process of watching women's studies falter in the 1990s. The story of women's studies suggests that our current and future contests over meaning and knowledge, and for freedom and equality, should probably avoid consolidating victories in the form of new degree-granting programs in the university. But it does not tell us what to do instead. Perhaps the present moment is one for considering where we have been so that we might, in a Nietzschean vein, *affirm our errors*. Perhaps it is a moment for thinking.

NOTES

Preface

1. Michel Foucault, "Two Lectures," *Power/Knowledge: Selected Interviews and Other Writings, 1972–1977*, ed. Colin Gordon (New York: Pantheon, 1980), 81.

Chapter One

Untimeliness and Punctuality: Critical Theory

in Dark Times

1. Michel Foucault, "What Is Critique?" in *The Political*, ed. David Ingram (Oxford: Blackwell, 2001), 193.

2. Walter Benjamin, "Theses on the Philosophy of History," in *Illuminations*, ed. Hannah Arendt, trans. Harry Zohn (New York: Schocken Books, 1968), thesis 6, 255.

3. See, for example, "The Uproar over Nader" by Alexander Cockburn and Jeffrey St. Clair, in *CounterPunch* 11.3 (February 1–15, 2004): 1, 4; and Todd S. Purdum, "Reasons to Run? Nader Says He Has Plenty," *New York Times*, March 31, 2004, p. A1, with ensuing letters to the editor.

4. *Temperate* derives from the Latin *temperare*, itself deriving from *tempus*, meaning the proper time or season.

5. "Schopenhauer as Educator," in *The Complete Works of Friedrich Nietzsche*, vol. 2, *Unfashionable Observations*, trans. Richard T. Gray (Stanford: Stanford University Press, 1995), 193, 196.

6. The Latin *cernere*, to sift, derives from *krinein*, "criticism," which shares the Greek root *kri-*.

7. Reinhart Koselleck, *Critique and Crisis: Enlightenment and the Pathogenesis of Modern Society* (Cambridge, MA: MIT Press, 1988), 103 (with n. 15).

8. I am indebted to an unpublished dissertation chapter by Tim Walters for this and several other insights into critique's etymology. Walters in turn relies heavily upon the research of Reinhart Koselleck in *Critique and Crisis*, as do I.

9. Koselleck, *Critique and Crisis*, 103.

10. In his discussion of the original meaning of critique in *What Is a Thing?* Heidegger makes this point quite strongly: "Critique is so little negative that it means the most positive of the positive, a separation and lifting out of the special that is at the same time, the decisive. . . . [O]nly as a consequence is it also a rejection of the commonplace and unsuitable" (trans. W. B. Barton, Jr., and Vera Deutsch [Chicago: Regnery Press, 1967], 119–20).

11. Kosseleck, *Critique and Crisis*, 104 n. 14.

12. There is no question that Truth becomes a nodal point of critique in modernity, even as critique takes Truth as one of its objects. Both sides of this paradox appear in Kant's famous declaration in the preface to the first edition of *Critique of Pure Reason*: "our age is the genuine age of criticism to which everything must submit" (trans. and ed. Paul Guyer and Allen W. Wood [Cambridge: Cambridge University Press, 1998], 100–101). For Kant, critique involves the submission of dogma to reason. For Hegel and Marx, too, critique is the activity through which religious and traditional prejudices are shed and Truth is left standing. Yet, as we know, these powerful Kantian and Hegelian weapons ultimately turn against the prize they aimed to capture. If truth is all that remains at the end of critique, then Kant's dictum—that *everything* must submit to critique—also ensures that Truth itself will be undone by critique.

13. Jacques Derrida, *Specters of Marx: The State of the Debt, the Work of Mourning, and the New International*, trans. Peggy Kamuf (New York: Routledge, 1994), 18.

14. Ibid., 13, 14.

15. One only need think here of George W. Bush's depiction of Iraq's possession of weapons of mass destruction as a wholly successful legitimating strategy for initiating a war.

16. William E. Connolly, *Neuropolitics: Thinking, Culture, Speed* (Minneapolis: University of Minnesota Press, 2002). While the entire book is concerned in part with the question of reconceiving time in late modernity, see especially chapters 6 and 7.

17. Sheldon Wolin, "What Time Is It?" *Theory and Event* 1.1 (1997): para. 4 (http://muse.jhu.edu/journals/theory_and_event/[restricted access]).

18. More precisely, Connolly says: "The acceleration of pace carries danger . . . but it also sets a condition of possibility for achievements that democrats and pluralists prize. The question for me, then, is not how to slow the world down, but how to work with and against a world moving faster than heretofore to promote a positive ethos of pluralism" (*Neuropolitics*, 143).

19. Fredric Jameson, *The Seeds of Time* (New York: Columbia University Press, 1994), 70–71.

20. Ibid., 71.

21. Friedrich Nietzsche, "At Noon" and "The Night Song" in *Thus Spoke Zarathustra*, in *The Portable Nietzsche*, trans. and ed. Walter Kaufmann (New York: Viking Press, 1968), 387–90, 217–19.

22. Benjamin, "Theses on the Philosophy of History," 262.

23. Thesis 17: "Historicism rightly culminates in universal history. Materialistic historiography differs from it as to method more clearly than from any other kind. Universal history has no theoretical armature. Its method is additive; it musters a mass of data to fill the homogeneous, empty time. Materialistic historiography, on the other hand, is based on a constructive principle" (ibid., 262).

24. Still from thesis 17: "Thinking involves not only the flow of thoughts, but their arrest as well. Where thinking suddenly stops in a configuration pregnant with tensions, it gives that configuration a shock, by which it crystallizes into a monad" (ibid., 262–63).

25. For more extended discussion of this point, see chapter 2 of my *Politics Out of History* (Princeton: Princeton University Press, 2001) and the introduction to *Left Legalism/Left Critique*, ed. Wendy Brown and Janet Halley (Durham, N.C.: Duke University Press, 2002).

26. Benjamin, "Theses on the Philosophy of History," 263.

27. Nietzsche, "Schopenhauer as Educator," 235; Wolin, "What Time Is It?"; Norman O. Brown, "A Reply to Herbert Marcuse," *commentary* 43.3 (March 1967): 83–87.

28. In "Politics as a Vocation," Weber famously argued that both an "ethic of ultimate ends" and an "absolute ethic" were inappropriate to politics: the former brooks any means to a chosen political end and the latter reverses this principle, cleaving to a principle of action (such as nonviolence) regardless of the consequences. Each eschews the medium of politics, which is violence, and the nature of political action, which is unintended consequences. Each also subscribes to what Weber called the infantile belief that the goodness of an action is related to the goodness of its intention or agent, when in fact "he who lets himself in for politics . . . contracts with diabolical powers." In place of an ethic of ultimate ends and an absolute ethic (of principled means), Weber substituted an ethic of responsibility, by which he meant the political actor is responsible, in advance of any action, for action's unpredictable effects and hence for the world one's actions may inadvertently bring into being. See *From Max Weber: Essays in Sociology*, ed. H. H. Gerth and C. Wright Mills (Oxford: Oxford University Press, 1946), 118–26.

29. Foucault, "What Is Critique?" 193.

Chapter Two

Political Idealization and Its Discontents

1. For extended consideration of this point, see my forthcoming book, *Regulating Aversion: Tolerance in the Age of Identity and Empire* (Princeton University Press, forthcoming), and especially chapter 4. "The Governmentality of Tolerance."

2. Precisely because of the limited scope of this essay's concern with dissent, it should not therefore be read as an endorsement of the Burkean injunction against challenging fundamental features of an established political collectivity or against calling for a fundamental transformation of the collectivity. One can legitimately argue, as an American, for a vision of America as a politically and economically decentralized, multicultural socialist democracy; just as one can argue, as an Israeli, for a vision of Israel as a democratic secular state. Of course there are those who would contend that these are no longer visions of America or Israel, but rather constitute their abolition. Samuel Huntington, for example, has famously argued that "a multicultural America is impossible because a non-Western America is not American. . . . [M]ulticulturalism at home threatens the United States and the West" (*The Clash of Civilizations and the Remaking of World Order* [New York: Simon and Schuster, 1996], 306). There is no way to settle the question of when critique is internal to the constitutive terms of a polity and when it is external, of when a particular vision extends the history of a nation and when it constitutes a rupture with that history, nor is it the purpose of this essay to pose or settle these questions.

3. Translations of the *Apology* and the *Crito*, by Hugh Tredennick, are from *The Collected Dialogues of Plato*, ed. Edith Hamilton and Huntington Cairns (Princeton: Princeton University Press, 1961).

4. Thus, Socrates explains why he could "not venture to come forward in public and advise the state" (*Apology* 31c), why, even when he was a senator, he went home rather than carry out a policy he considered illegal; and why he refused to carry out the orders of the oligarchy even as he risked death for doing so.

5. Dana Villa, *Socratic Citizenship* (Princeton: Princeton University Press, 2001), 22–23.

6. Ibid., 23.

7. Ibid., 6.

8. Michel Foucault develops a notion of critique as virtue in his essay "What Is Critique?" See also the essay by Judith Butler on Foucault's essay, "What Is Critique? An Essay on Foucault's Virtue." Both are in *The Political*, ed. David Ingram (Oxford: Blackwell, 2001).

9. Michel Foucault, "Governmentality" in *The Foucault Effect: Studies in Governmentality*, ed. Graham Burchell, Colin Gordon, and Peter Miller (Chicago: University of Chicago Press, 1991), 92.

10. At times, this distinction may be so fine as to be almost unsustainable. It does not turn upon a putative difference between words and actions. Nor does it turn upon the difference between questioning the laws and disobeying them; legal authority can be more radically undermined by the former than the latter. Rather, as I will argue in what follows, I think it turns upon avowal of attachment to the object of critique and the limit this avowal poses to the destructive force of the critique.

11. *Group Psychology and the Analysis of the Ego*, in the *Standard Edition of the Complete Psychological Works of Sigmund Freud*, trans. and ed. James Strachey, 24 vols. (London: Hogarth Press, 1953–64), 18:111–12. The *Standard Edition* is hereafter cited as *SE*, and *Group Psychology* is hereafter cited parenthetically in the text as *GP*.

12. One of Freud's best examples here helps us understand not only political patriotic fervor but the phenomenon of thousands of screaming teenage girls clutching each other in shared delirium at a pop concert: "We have only to think of the troop of women and girls, all of them in love in an enthusiastically sentimental way, who crowd round a singer or pianist after his performance. It would certainly be easy for each of them to be jealous of the rest; but, in the face of their numbers and the consequent impossibility of their reaching the aim of their love, they renounce it, and instead of pulling out one another's hair, they act as a united group, do homage to the hero of the occasion with their common actions, and would probably be glad to have a share of *his* flowing locks" (*GP*, 120).

13. Sigmund Freud, *Civilization and Its Discontents*, in *SE* 21:114.

14. In *Future of an Illusion*, Freud argues: "The narcissistic satisfaction provided by the cultural ideal is also among the forces which are successful in combating the hostility to culture within the cultural unit. This satisfaction can be shared in not only by the favoured classes, which enjoy the benefits of the culture, but also by the suppressed ones, since the right to despise the people outside it compensates them for the wrongs they suffer within their own unit. No doubt one is a wretched plebeian, harassed by debts and military service; but, to make up for it, one is a Roman citizen, one has one's share in the task of ruling other nations and dictating their laws" in *SE* 21:13.

15. Sigmund Freud, *Totem and Taboo*, trans. James Strachey (New York: Norton, 1950), 49; hereafter cited parenthetically in the text as *TT*.

16. Slavoj Žižek, *The Sublime Object of Ideology* (London: Verso, 1989), 105.

17. Rey Chow, *Ethics after Idealism: Theory—Culture—Ethnicity—Reading* (Bloomington: Indiana University Press, 1998), 42.

18. Ibid.

19. Žižek, *Sublime Object of Ideology*, 106.

20. Chow, *Ethics after Idealism*, 43.

21. Žižek's exploration of the hidden work of symbolic identification in legitimating a regime focuses on totalitarianism. However, for Žižek totalitarianism is not opposed to the ordinary workings of ideology in modern Western states, but rather is its strong version, or more precisely its cartoon version.

22. Michael Ignatieff, "Nationalism and Toleration," in *The Politics of Toleration: Tolerance and Intolerance in Modern Life*, ed. Susan Mendus (Edinburgh: Edinburgh University Press, 1999), 81.

CHAPTER THREE

NEOLIBERALISM AND THE END OF LIBERAL DEMOCRACY

1. *Governmentality* is a rich term that Foucault defines as the "conduct of conduct" (Colin Gordon, "Government Rationality: An Introduction," in *The Foucault Effect: Studies in Governmentality*, ed. Graham Burchell, Colin Gordon, and Peter Miller [Chicago: University of Chicago Press, 1991], 48). The term is also intended to signify the modern importance of *governing* over ruling and the critical role of *mentality* in governing, as opposed to the notion that power and ideas are separate phenomena. Governmentality moves away from sovereign and state-centered notions of political power (though it does not eschew the state as a site of governmentality), from the division between violence and law, and from a distinction between ideological and material power. Finally, governmentality features state formation of subjects rather than state control of subjects; put slightly differently, it emphasizes control achieved through formation rather than through repression or punishment. This being said, note that my account of governmentality differs somewhat from those of Colin Gordon and Nikolas Rose, both of whom have worked extensively on Foucault's lectures on governmentality, and differs as well from ways it has been taken up by other theorists. As is often the case with Foucault's ideas—think of biopower, resistance, power/knowledge, arts of the self—the notion of governmentality is both extremely theoretically fecund and woefully underspecified. Perhaps it could not be the former without being the latter.

2. Michel Foucault, *Naissance de la biopolitique: Cours au Collège de France (1978–1979)*, ed. Michel Senellart (Paris: Gallimard, 2004), appeared too late to be consulted for this work.

3. Thomas Lemke, "'The birth of bio-politics': Michel Foucault's Lecture at the Collège de France on Neo-liberal Governmentality," *Economy and Society* 30.2 (May 2001): 190–207; this article is hereafter cited parenthetically in the text as Lemke. Lemke and Foucault emphasize not only the continuities but also the differences between the German *Ordo*-liberals and the neoliberalism of the Chicago School. However, I will not be attending to these differences as I consider the implications of neoliberal governmentality. The most significant difference appears to be in the degree of support for the market each judges to be required by political regulations and social interventions. Both focus on the market, but "the *Ordo*-liberals . . . pursued the idea of governing society in the name of the economy [while] the U.S. neo-liberals attempt to re-define the social [and political] sphere as a form of the economic domain" (Lemke, 197–98). Thus, the former regard the economy as requiring political intervention and determining its nature, while the latter recast the economic as defining the entire sphere of human action and institutions, from individual behavior to government rationality.

4. The term *liberal* could not be more confused today, not only because of its different economic and political valences and its variable historical meanings, but also because at this moment in the United States, the standard electoral party opposition between liberal (as in liberalizing) and conservative (as in conserving) has collapsed. The Bush administration agenda is charged with being "radical" by liberals, an agenda that in turn positions Democrats as seeking to "conserve" welfare state policies and civil liberties against those (on the Right) who would "revolutionize" them. Moreover, as the Democratic Party struggles to recapture an American majority, some leading Democrats have joined in the right-wing practice of treating the appellation *liberal* as tantamount to Left, and hence "outside the mainstream."

5. Neoliberalism and neoconservatism are quite different, not least because the former functions as a political rationality while the latter remains an ideology (despite significant overlap in constituency and issues). Adherents of both, for example, oppose most aspects of the welfare state. But there are also tensions: neoconservatism's strong moral positions—on abortion, homosexuality, the family, etc.—have nothing to do with neoliberalism and actually fly in the face of the economic rationality that neoliberalism promulgates at the social level. This essay is concerned entirely with neoliberalism, but an investigation of the interplay of neoliberalism and neoconservatism is certainly in order, especially because the reigning Republicans are neocons. It would also be interesting to think about how, given the high moral tone of the neocons, amoral neoliberal rationality becomes part of the arsenal of tactics and strategy for advancing a neocon agenda—from ruthless calculation to "dirty tricks" like manipulating intelligence.

6. See Nicos Poulantzas, *Political Power and Social Classes*, trans. Timothy O'Hagan (London: Verso, 1975); Jürgen Habermas, *Legitimation Crisis*, trans. Thomas McCarthy (Boston: Beacon, 1975); and James O'Connor, *The Fiscal Crisis of the State* (New York: St. Martin's Press, 1973). As thinkers giving what was then called the "structuralist" response to cruder "instrumentalist" accounts of the capitalist state, all argued that whenever the state was required to ostentatiously intervene on behalf of capital (whether through overt bailouts and subsidies or slightly more covertly through policies that favored it), the state by tipping its hand ran the risk of a "legitimation crisis." That is, at such moments, the state revealed itself as a "capitalist" state, while its legitimacy depended on its perceived independence from social and economic powers. This is the criterion for legitimacy that neoliberalism overcomes by casting the state as an extension of the market—a legitimate servant of the market, an aspect of the market, or a form of the market.

7. Occasionally, this framing reaches parodic levels, as was the case in the Pentagon plan (ultimately nixed by the Senate Armed Services Committee) for setting up an online trading market to predict terrorist attacks. The goal of the scheme was to "improve the prediction and prevention of events by using the

expertise of the open market instead of relying only on government agencies," since, the Defense Department argued, "research indicates that markets are extremely efficient, effective and timely aggregators of dispersed and even hidden information." The plan involved setting up a futures market in which traders would make money if a terrorist event they bet on actually happened. Aside from its tastelessness, apparently the Department of Defense Advanced Research Projects Unit that designed the project had forgotten to reckon with the simple matter pointed out by Senate Democratic leader Tom Daschle: "this program could provide an incentive actually to commit acts of terrorism." However, Merli Baroudi, director of risk services for the England-based Economist Intelligence Unit, which provided data for the project, defended the plan as simply "trying to gather insights of people in a cost effective way." Many economists, political advisors, and political pundits concurred. (All quotation are drawn from "Pentagon Axes Online Terror Bets," *BBC News*, July 29, 2003, http://news.bbc.co.uk/1/hi/world/americas/3106559.stm [accessed January 2005].)

8. Sheldon Wolin calls attention to George W. Bush's urge to citizens to "shop, fly, and spend" at the outset of the war on terrorism, a supplication that contrasts sharply with the more conventional rallying of the citizenry around a war effort—asking for civic support and individual sacrifice (Wolin, "Brave New World," *Theory and Event* 5.4 [2002]; http://muse.jhu.edu/journals/theory_and_event/[restricted access]).

9. I recall an episode from my graduate student years at Princeton University: In the early 1980s, a Princeton senior had already been admitted to Harvard Law School when she was caught cheating—plagiarizing, I think—in a Spanish literature class. The student was given an F in the class but Harvard Law was also informed of the event by a Princeton dean and thereupon withdrew its offer of admission. The student's family sued Princeton, on the basis that the student's career had been damaged beyond what was appropriate to the magnitude of her error. Though the suit struck many of us as astonishing in its shameless valorization of economic over moral values in a liberal arts academic setting, it is now clear that we were simply behind the times.

10. In a press conference just prior to the invasion of Afghanistan, Bush dismissed one reporter's probing with the remark "I'll let others work out the legalities," forthrightly implying that law did not represent principles that ought to frame policy but was something to be gotten around or manipulated to suit a preestablished aim. Bush responded similarly to the 2003 Supreme Court decision in *Lawrence* that overturned state sodomy laws, stating when questioned about the ruling that "our lawyers are currently working on the question" of how best to secure marriage as an exclusively heterosexual institution.

11. Michael Bleyzer, quoted in Tim Shorrock "Selling (Off) Iraq: How to 'Privatize' a Country and Make Millions," *The Nation*, June 23, 2003, p. 13. Bleyzer, a former Exxon executive now running a private equity firm, has briefed U.S. officials, including Defense Secretary Donald Rumsfeld, on Iraq's political-economic future, and co-authored with Robert McFarlane a

commentary in the *Wall Street Journal* titled "Taking Iraq Private" (January 27, 2003, p. A10).

12. The American-based corporation DynCorp International has a $50 million contract with the State Department to provide "law enforcement" in postwar Iraq (Shorrock, "Selling (Off) Iraq," 13).

13. See, for example, Thomas L. Friedman, "Winning the Real War" (op-ed), *New York Times*, July 16, 2003, p. A19, which dismisses Bush's "hyping of the W.M.O. issue" as relatively unimportant.

14. San Dillon "Out of Money, Some School Districts in Oregon End the Year Early," *New York Times*, May 24, 2003, p. A13.

15. Dean E. Murphy, "San Francisco Protest Brings Debate on Wages of Din," *New York Times*, June 23, 2003, p. A14.

16. In a recent *Nation* article, Sheldon S. Wolin proposed calling the current organization of power in the United States "inverted totalitarianism" ("Inverted Totalitarianism: How the Bush Regime Is Effecting the Transformation to a Fascist-like State, *"The Nation*, May 19, 2003, pp. 13–14). While the description Wolin offers is commensurate with many aspects of the neoliberal political rationality described here, I am not persuaded that Wolin's term captures the novelty of this political form as a *rationality* that is independent of traditional forms of *rule*. What strikes me as so useful about Foucault's notion of governmentality is precisely that it apprehends the extent to which rationality governs without recourse to overt rule—or, more precisely, the manner in which it governs through norms and rules rather than rule.

17. *Mourning and Melancholia*, in *The Standard Edition of the Complete Psychological Works of Sigmund Freud*, trans. and ed. James Strachey, 24 vols. (London: Hogarth, 1953–64), 14:252.

18. Lemke notes that for the Chicago School neoliberals, "a criminal is not a psychologically deficient person or a biological degenerate. . . . The criminal is a rational-economic individual who invests, expects a certain profit and risks making a loss. From the angle of *homo œconomicus* there is no fundamental difference between a murder and a parking offence. It is the task of the penal system to respond to a supply of crimes, and punishment is one means of constraining the negative externalities of specific actions. . . . For the neoliberals, crime is no longer located outside the market model, but is instead one market among others" (199).

CHAPTER FOUR

AT THE EDGE: THE FUTURE OF POLITICAL THEORY

1. Foucault's return to Kant's question "Was Ist Aufklärung?" is a rich instance of the strategy of admixture here. See Foucault's essay by this title in *The Foucault Reader*, ed. Paul Rabinow (New York: Pantheon, 1984), 32–50.

2. Giorgio Agamben, *Means without End: Notes on Politics*, trans. Vincenzo Binetti and Cesare Casarino (Minneapolis: University of Minnesota Press, 2000), 113.

3. Here I refer to the division of political theory into distinct strains: liberal democratic thought, Arendtian-inflected democratic thought, (liberal) communitarian thought, neo-Nietzschean and poststructuralist thought, Habermassian thought, Straussian thought, Marxist thought, moral political philosophy, psychoanalytic thought, and still others harder to name. While there is crossover terrain and there are also crossover artists, for the most part each strain has its own subcanon, its own roster of stars and rising stars, its own groundbreaking and self-endorsed monographs and anthologies, its own newsletters and conferences.

4. Some of the most interesting contemporary philosophers of the political reject both of these formulations of the political. See, for example, Jacques Rancière's "Ten Theses on Politics," published in English in *Theory and Event* 5.3 (2001), at http://muse.jhu.edu/journals/theory_and_event/(restricted access), or consider Giorgio Agamben's recent insistence that "politics is a force field, an intensity, not a substance" and that this force field is delimited by the "friend/enemy" relation (seminar, Princeton University, October 15, 2001). I find these accounts provocative, if not fully convincing, and above all appreciate them for inciting theoretical conversation about what we mean by politics and the political today.

5. The general intellectual impoverishment of political theory on these developments is apparent in a wide range of topics. For example, in a seminar I recently taught on political theories of tolerance, an anthropology graduate student remarked that culture is more reified and less theorized in the work of most contemporary democratic theorists addressing multiculturalism than it was for anthropologists in the nineteenth century. Treated as a kind of primal, transhistorical, and subrational good, assumed to be especially cherished and valued by oppressed minorities, culture is generally counterposed to liberalism and cosmopolitanism, both of which are generally presumed to be cultureless.

6. At the moment when the very possibility of apprehending the "real world" has been challenged by postfoundationalist analysis and by the insistence that all description is embodied in discourse, every utterance can now potentially qualify as a theoretical one.

7. These thoughts were developed in the context of a seminar on *Jean Laplanche: Seduction, Translation and the Drives* offered by Judith Butler at Princeton University in November 2001. Working from my notes, I am uncertain which of these thoughts are Butler's, which are her reading of Laplanche's remarks about the nature of theory, and which are my own thoughts in response to Butler and Laplanche. Nor has she been able to answer this question. So this paragraph stands as collaboratively written, if unintentionally so.

CHAPTER FIVE

FREEDOM'S SILENCES

1. See Michel Foucault, *The History of Sexuality*, vol. 1, *An Introduction*, trans. Robert Hurley (New York: Vintage, 1980); Joan Scott, "'Experience,'" in *Feminists Theorize the Political*, ed. Judith Butler and Joan Scott (New York: Routledge, 1992), 22–40; and Shoshana Felman and Dori Laub, *Testimony: Crises of Witnessing in Literature, Psychoanalysis, and History* (New York: Routledge, 1992).

2. Catharine MacKinnon, *Toward a Feminist Theory of the State* (Cambridge, Mass.: Harvard University Press, 1989).

3. On this point, and for an exceptionally thoughtful meditation on the feminist politics of voice that at times parallels my own, see Valerie Hazel, "Disjointed Articulations: The Politics of Voice and Jane Campion's *The Piano*," *Women's Studies Journal* 10.2 (September 1994), 27–40.

4. This potential would appear to be more visible and cautionary among African Americans and other racially marked groups in the United States than among whites. Consider, as popular examples, the "we don't talk about it in public" (that is, a white public) attitude voiced by many African American women about sexual harassment and spousal abuse following the Anita Hill and O. J. Simpson spectacles. Or consider, as an example in fiction, Alice Walker's "Advancing Luna and Ida B. Wells," a story in which an African American woman feels consigned to silence about the alleged rape of her white co-worker by an African American acquaintance. In both cases, there is deep cognizance of the racist regulatory discourses in which the "voicing of truth" would be taken up.

5. Foucault, *History of Sexuality*, 100–101.

6. Ibid., 101.

7. Agnes Lugo-Ortiz, "Community at Its Limits: Orality, Law, Silence, and the Homosexual Body in Luis Rafael Sanchez's 'Jum!'" in *¿Entiendes? Queer Readings, Hispanic Writings*, ed. Emilie L. Bergmann and Paul Julian Smith (Durham: Duke University Press, 1995), 115–36; and M. Jacqui Alexander, "Redrafting Morality: The Postcolonial State and the Sexual Offences Bill of Trinidad and Tobago," in *Third World Women and the Politics of Feminism*, ed. Chandra T. Mohanty, Anna Russo, and Lourdes Torres (Bloomington: Indiana University Press, 1991), 133–52.

8. Lugo-Ortiz, "Community at Its Limits," 131.

9. Foucault, *History of Sexuality*, 32, 31. That Foucault made a significant "mistake" in his infamous account of the nineteenth-century farmhand who was arrested, interned, and then elaborately analyzed by medical and psychological experts for "obtaining a few caresses from a little girl" is beyond question. When he remarks on "the pettiness of it all . . . [of] this everyday occurrence in the life of village sexuality, these inconsequential bucolic pleasures,"

certainly he is describing the scene from the point of view of power; one sur-
mises that the "bucolic pleasures" were the man's and one is left to wonder
about their "inconsequentiality" for the girl. And yet, this mistake may also be
a productive one. What if, despite the coercion or the conditions of power that
put the young girl in this scene, it was not a dramatic or traumatic event for
her? What if, however coerced or unpleasant, the scene was not emotionally or
physically devastating but was as banal in its unpleasantness as the act of
cleaning the chicken coop? And what if this scenario is nearly impossible for
us to contemplate because our discourses of sexuality, gender, childhood, personhood, and molestation together prohibit its possibility? Again, the point is
not that Foucault's description is unproblematic, but that its problematic character might be made useful (rather than the occasion for its dismissal) if it pro-
vokes us to imagine unequal or unwanted sexual encounters outside of the
discourses currently organizing them, and thus to contemplate when these
discourses immiserate rather than emancipate.

10. Still, there would appear to be a strangely modernist narrative at play in
Foucault's account of the innocent days prior to power, a narrative in which
"the fall" takes the form of being brought into regulatory discourse. Ironically,
particularly in the story of the molesting villager, feminist analysis provides an
easy antidote to the notion that there was pleasure and delight all around
prior to sexuality's subjection by medical and juridical discourse.

And yet, we might ask whether certain feminist discourses about sexual
abuse are not themselves constructive of the abuse, in the sense that they fashion an ambiguous experience *as* abuse. May we really be certain that every
childhood sexual act—with a sibling or an adult—was a traumatic or abusive
one prior to the moment of its exposure to a moral discourse? When the sex is
not coerced or imposed, is not the shame about the experience a great part of
its injury, and is not this shame potentially imposed through discourses surrounding or retroactively imposed on the experience rather than those intrinsic to the experience? If feminist discourses about sexuality have rendered
such questioning taboo, would this not be an instance of feminist discourse silencing its own subjects?

11. On Foucault's formulation of freedom as a "practice," see Paul Rabinow's
interview with Foucault, "Space, Knowledge and Power," in *The Foucault
Reader*, ed. Rabinow (New York: Pantheon, 1984), 245.

12. Michel Foucault, "The Minimalist Self," in *Politics, Philosophy, Culture:
Interviews and Other Writings, 1977–1984*, ed. Lawrence D. Kritzman (New
York: Routledge, 1988), 4.

13. Toni Morrison, *Lecture and Speech of Acceptance, Upon the Award of the
Nobel Prize for Literature, Delivered in Stockholm on the Seventh of December, Nine-
teen Hundred and Ninety-Three* (New York: Knopf, 1994), 13–14, 16.

14. Michel Foucault, "Two Lectures," in *Power/Knowledge: Selected Interviews
and Other Writings, 1972–1977*, ed. Colin Gordon (New York: Pantheon, 1980), 86.

15. For a general discussion of premenstrual syndrome and the law, see Lee Solomon, "Premenstrual Syndrome: The Debate Surrounding Criminal Defense," *Maryland Law Review* 54 (1995): 571–93; for battered women's syndrome, see Lenore Walker, *The Battered Women's Syndrome* (New York: Springer, 1984), and *State v. Kelly*, 97 NJ 178, 478 A2d 364 (1984), holding that battered women's syndrome has sufficient scientific basis that expert testimony on it must be admissible); and for the Meese Commission's conclusions, see U.S. Department of Justice, *Attorney General's Commission on Pornography* (Washington, D.C.: GPO, 1986), 322–52.

16. This analysis is more fully pursued in my *States of Injury: Power and Freedom in Late Modernity* (Princeton: Princeton University Press, 1995), chapter 5.

17. Primo Levi, *The Drowned and the Saved*, trans. Raymond Rosenthal (New York: Summit, 1988), 93–94.

18. Adrienne Rich, "Twenty-One Love Poems," in *The Dream of a Common Language: Poems, 1974–1977* (New York: Norton, 1978), 29.

19. Note that the verb *to drown* is not only both passive and active—"she drowned in the river," "he drowned her in the bathtub"—but can also connote a condition from which one can return as well as a final state, one that terminates in death. There is a life-and-death difference between *drowning* and *drowned*. There is a vanishing at work in both; but Levi, it would seem, wants to capture this vanishing without giving it final say, without allowing it to turn into vanquishing. Thus, the drowning may become the saved . . . or the drowned.

20. Levi, *The Drowned and the Saved*, 76.

21. Ibid., 24 (emphasis added).

22. Hannah Arendt, *The Human Condition* (Chicago: University of Chicago Press, 1958), 51.

23. Patricia Williams, *The Alchemy of Race and Rights* (Cambridge, Mass.: Harvard University Press, 1991), 236 (emphasis added).

Chapter Six

Feminism Unbound: Revolution, Mourning, Politics

1. This paper was the keynote lecture for the United Kingdom Women's Studies Network Conference, "Beyond Sex and Gender: The Future of Women's Studies?" September 19–21, 2002 in Belfast, Ireland.

2. "The dead seize the living!" Karl Marx, preface to the First German Edition, *Capital*, vol. 1, trans. Samuel Moore and Edward Aveling, ed. Frederick Engels (1887; reprint, New York: International Publishers, 1967), 9.

3. Hannah Arendt, *On Revolution* (London: Viking Press, 1965), 29, 34.

4. Ibid., 50–51.

5. See Karl Marx, "On the Jewish Question," in *The Marx-Engels Reader*, ed. Robert Tucker, 2nd ed. (New York: Norton, 1978), 26–52.

6. "What from [the French Revolution onward] has been irrevocable, and what the agents and spectators of revolution immediately recognized as such, was that the public realm—reserved, as far as memory could reach, to those who *were* free, namely carefree of all the worries that are connected with life's necessity, with bodily needs—should offer its space and its light to this immense majority who are not free because they are driven by daily needs. . . . The notion of an irresistible movement, which the nineteenth century soon was to conceptualize into the idea of historical necessity, echoes from beginning to end through the pages of the French Revolution" (Arendt, *On Revolution*, 48).

7. Gillian Rose, *Mourning Becomes the Law: Philosophy and Representation* (Cambridge: Cambridge University Press, 1966), 125–29.

8. Ibid., 130.

9. Karl Marx, *Manifesto of the Communist Party*, in *The Marx-Engels Reader*, 477.

10. See Herbert Marcuse, *One Dimensional Man: Studies in the Ideology of Advanced Industrial Society* (Boston: Beacon Press, 1964).

11. See Miglena Nikolchina, "The Seminar: *Mode d'emploi*. Impure Spaces in the Light of Late Totalitarianism," *Differences: A Journal of Cultural Feminist Studies* 13.1 (Spring 2002): 96–127.

12. In addition to the belief that we could become new women and men, that gender could be made differently, revolutionary feminism carried the conviction that masculinist values in every venue could be uprooted and replaced. These included values that overtly governed and produced gender but also those constituting the historical anatomy of war, diplomacy, business, sexuality, the liberal state, the family, public and private, and more. Revolutionary feminism's aim to transform the nature of public and economic life, and not simply to obtain an equal place for women in it, is routinely occluded in the endless spate of writing that ties feminism's current lack of cachet to its failure to address the difficulty of balancing work and family. (Most recent in the genre is an essay by Kay S. Hymowitz in which she attributes not just the decline but the *death* of feminism to its failure to reckon with "biology and ordinary bourgeois longings"; see "The End of Herstory," *City* 12.3 [Summer 2002]; available at www.city-journal.org/html/issue_12_3.html [accessed January 2005].) But feminism in a revolutionary mode never intended to address this difficulty; rather, it sought to transform the order that made balancing work and family women's problem in the first place and impossible in the second. It did not ask how to solve this problem within existing parameters but rather asked what arrangements of work, love, and kinship would offer a more richly humane satisfaction of a variety of human desires and needs. The fact that this utopian impulse is now routinely (mis)cast as feminists' eschewal of fixed

psychic and biological coordinates testifies to how thoroughly incomprehensible, indeed, unthinkable, a revolutionary political spirit and *worldview* are today, how thoroughly both have vanished from the popular imagination, and at the same time how relentlessly reified and naturalized existing social arrangements have become.

CHAPTER SEVEN

THE IMPOSSIBILITY OF WOMEN'S STUDIES

1. While it is true that debates about "fundamentals" pervade many disciplines, I think that in most it is possible both to acknowledge the fictional character of the field *and* to venture arguments about what constitutes a good undergraduate education in those fields. For example, I would argue that any undergraduate obtaining a bachelor of arts in politics or political science in this country should have a basic grasp of (1) international relations in the era of nation-states and globalization, (2) U.S. political institutions, (3) one or two other political systems, (4) political economy, (5) social movements as sources of modern political upheaval and change, and (6) the history of political theory. This is a contestable list, and it also does not specify how this basic grasp is to be procured. However, what concerns me here is the disconcerting fact of my inability, and my colleagues' inability, to conjure a similar list for women's studies about which to begin arguing.

2. Two recent anecdotes from feminist colleagues at other universities sharpen this point. (1) A feminist scholar at a public university was asked to remove her course, "Introduction to Sexualities," from the women's studies curriculum on the grounds that its subject matter was sex, not gender. (2) The director of women's studies at a research university was seeking to convert her steadily declining program into one on gender and sexuality, for which there was abundant student demand and faculty interest. But in the process, she met with intense resistance from colleagues who feared a loss of focus on women, and especially women of color, in the revamped program.

3. The formulations offered by Kimberle Crenshaw, Aida Hurtado, and Patricia Hill Collins are useful for thinking about the difficult place of entry for black women into legal discourse (Crenshaw, "Demarginalizing the Intersection of Race and Sex: A Black Feminist Critique of Antidiscrimination Doctrine, Feminist Theory, and Antiracist Politics," *University of Chicago Legal Forum* [1989]: 139–66), or the difficulty of making feminist political coalitions among women of color and white women (Hurtado, "Relating to Privilege: Seduction and Rejection in the Subordination of White Women and Women of Color," *Signs* 14.4 [1989]: 833–54), or the distinctiveness of black women's

thought and political practice (Collins, *Black Feminist Thought: Knowledge, Consciousness, and the Politics of Empowerment* [New York: Routledge, 1981]; quotation, 42). However, these projects should not be confused with the project of offering an account or description of subject formation.

What happens if Crenshaw's notion of "intersectionality" is used to explain the subject formation or even subject position of black women in the United States, as opposed to the conundrums faced by black women attempting to make use of antidiscrimination law and forced to choose between racial or gendered standing? Imagine that someone lives in the country, and one day a set of roads is laid down adjacent to her house. One road is named Gender, the other is named Race, the woman's house is at their intersection, and, for purposes of having an address, she is asked to choose which one she lives on. Whether she chooses one or the other, or whether she insists that she lives at their intersection, these roads impose an address, and the address will have its consequences, but neither the roads nor the address radically constitute this subject nor provide an account of such constitution. The woman is not an intersection, nor is she intersectional; rather, she lives at an intersection of naming in the law, as do most people. "Intersectionality" describes a phenomena of address and interpellation, and offers a potential strategy for navigating it. Black women as such are not "intersectional"; rather, their legal position is.

4. Thus, to consider the making of gender through sexuality without reference to the more general regime of sexuality Foucault depicts in *The History of Sexuality* (MacKinnon's mistake) is just as myopic as formulating the terms of that regime with little or no reference to gender (Foucault's mistake). See Michel Foucault, *The History of Sexuality*, vol. 1, *An Introduction*, trans. Robert Hurley (New York: Vintage, 1980); Catharine MacKinnon, *Feminism Unmodified: Discourses on Life and Law* (Cambridge, Mass.: Harvard University Press, 1987).

5. Judith Butler, "Regulation," in *Critical Terms in Gender Studies*, ed. Gilbert Herdt and Catharine R. Stimpson (Chicago: University of Chicago Press, forthcoming).

6. "The individual is an effect of power, and at the same time . . . it is the element of its articulation. The individual which power has constituted is at the same time its vehicle" (Michel Foucault, "Two Lectures," in *Power/Knowledge: Selected Interviews and Other Writings, 1972–1977*, ed. Colin Gordon [New York: Pantheon, 1980], 98).

7. It should be underscored that not all who travel under the sign of "critical race theory" subscribe to the view of rights most notably articulated by Patricia Williams in *The Alchemy of Race and Rights* (Cambridge, Mass.: Harvard University Press, 1991), and Robert A. Williams, Jr., in an earlier article, "Taking Rights Aggressively: The Perils and Promise of Critical Legal Theory for Peoples of Color," *Law and Inequality* 5.1 (1987): 103–34.

8. For a more complete development of this point, see my "Rights and Losses" in *States of Injury: Power and Freedom in Late Modernity* (Princeton: Princeton University Press, 1995), 96–134, and "Suffering Rights as Paradoxes," *Constellations* 7.2 (June 2000): 208–29.

9. Some might argue that miscegenation laws functioned in this way. However, miscegenation laws did not criminalize the racially marked subject as such in the way that sodomy laws do, but rather regulated the sexuality of such subjects.

10. It should be noted that the monological axes of analysis I am deploying here both underscore and fail the point made above, that modes of subject production operate through different trajectories and modalities of subjection, and must be subjected to distinctive modes of analysis, yet cannot be extricated from one another in living subjects. Thus, to say as I did here, that "there is no equivalent to the crucial place of reproductive rights for women's equality in defining the parameters of racial freedom, or ending the stigma for minority sexual orientation," elides the fact that racism and heterosexism operate in part through the distinct lack of reproductive freedom for peoples of color and homosexuals. Yet to presume that this lack functions in the same way *as* racism and heterosexism as it does *as* sexism is precisely to colonize racism and heterosexism with a feminist analysis, a colonization feminists have been engaging in for too long. This is the move that Catharine MacKinnon makes with regard to thinking about the place of women of color and racism in pornography, presumably to establish that her feminist analysis is also an analysis of race and racism (see MacKinnon, *Only Words* [Cambridge, Mass.: Harvard University Press, 1996]). But it strikes me as an argument that is in bad faith as well as analytically impoverished.

11. Janet Halley and Kendall Thomas, in, for example, their respective readings of *Bowers v. Hardwick*, are notable exceptions in the field of queer jurisprudence. See Halley, "Reasoning about Sodomy: Act and Identity in and after *Bowers v. Hardwick*," *Virginia Law Review* 79 (1993): 1721–80; Thomas, "The Eclipse of Reason: A Rhetorical Reading of *Bowers v. Hardwick*," *Virginia Law Review* 79 (1993): 1805–51.

INDEX